The Series *THE ORTHODOX FAITH* is intended to provide basic, comprehensive information on the faith and life of the Orthodox Church for the average reader. It consists of four handbooks.

Volume I on *DOCTRINE* contains three sections: the sources of Christian doctrine, the main doctrines of the Orthodox Church presented by way of commentary on the Nicene Creed, and an explanation of the doctrine of the Holy Trinity.

Volume II on *WORSHIP* contains five sections: the church building, vestments and symbols; the sacraments; the daily cycle of worship; the church year with its fasts and feasts; and the divine liturgy.

Volume III on *BIBLE AND CHURCH HISTORY* contains one section on the contents and interpretation of the Bible, and one section on the history of the Church, emphasizing the main theological, liturgical and spiritual developments of each century.

Volume IV on *SPIRITUALITY* deals with the main themes of Christian Life: prayer, fasting, repentance, the virtues, witness in the world and communion with God.

THE ORTHODOX FAITH

volume i

doc-
trine

by Father Thomas Hopko

Illustrated by John Matusiak

AN ELEMENTARY HANDBOOK
ON THE ORTHODOX CHURCH

Number 1 of a series in THE ORTHODOX FAITH

ISBN 0-86642-036-3
1971 — First Printing
1976 — Second Edition (Revised)
© 1981 — Second Edition (Reprint)
1984 — Second Edition (Reprint)
DRE — Orthodox Church of America

Published by: The Department of Religious Education
The Orthodox Church in America

1981   New York

CONTENTS

1

THE SOURCES
OF CHRISTIAN
DOCTRINE

Revelation

Every morning at its Matins Service the Orthodox Church proclaims: **"God is the Lord and has revealed Himself unto us; blessed is He who comes in the name of the Lord."** (Psalm 118:26-27) The first foundation of Christian doctrine is found in this biblical line: **God has revealed Himself to us.**

God has shown Himself to His creatures. He has not disclosed His very innermost being, for this innermost essence of God cannot be grasped by creatures. But God has truly shown what men can see and understand of His divine nature and will.

The fullness and perfection of God's self-revelation is found in His Son Jesus Christ, the fulfillment of the gradual and partial revelation of God in the Old Testament. Jesus is the one truly **"blessed...who comes in the name of the Lord."**

The first title given to Jesus by the people is that of **Rabbi**, which literally means **teacher**. In the English New Testament the word **Master** also issued in relation to Jesus in the sense of one who teaches, such as a schoolmaster or holder of a master's degree. Jesus' followers are also called **disciples**, which literally means students or pupils.

Jesus came to men first of all as the Teacher sent from God. He teaches the will of God and makes God known to men. He reveals fully--as fully as men can grasp—the mysteries of the Kingdom of God.

The coming of Jesus as teacher is one aspect of his being Christ the Messiah. The word **Christ** in Greek is the word for the Hebrew **Messiah** which means the Anointed of God. For when the messiah would come, it was foretold, men would be **"taught by God."** (Isaiah 54:13; John 6:45)

Jesus comes to men as the divine teacher. He claimed on many occasions that his words were those of God. He spoke as **"one having authority"** not like the normal Jewish teachers. (Matthew 7:29) And he accused those who rejected his teachings as rejecting God Himself.

> He who believes in me, believes not in me but in him who sent me. And he who sees me sees Him who sent me. I have come as light into the world ... for I have not spoken on my own authority; the Father who sent me has himself given me commandment what to speak. What I say, therefore, I say as the Father has bidden me.
> (John 12:44-50)

Jesus taught men not only by his words, but also by his actions; and indeed by his very own person. He referred to himself as the Truth (John 14:6) and as the Light (John 8:12). He showed himself not merely to be speaking God's words, but to be himself the Living **Word of God** in human flesh, the **Logos** who is eternal and uncreated, but who has become man as Jesus of Nazareth in order to make God known to the world.

> In the beginning was the Word (Logos) and the Word was with God and the Word was God. He was in the beginning with God; all things were made through him, and without him was not anything made that was made.
>
> In him was life and the life was the light of men. The light shines in the darkness, and the darkness has not overcome it.
>
> The true light that enlightens every man was coming into the world. He was in the world, and the world was made through him, yet the world knew him not.
>
> And the Word became flesh and dwelt among us, full of grace and truth; we have beheld his glory, glory as of the only-begotten Son from the Father.
>
> And from his fullness have we all received, grace upon grace. For the law came through Moses; grace and truth came through Jesus Christ.

No one has ever seen God; the only-begotten Son who is in the bosom of the Father, he has made him known. (See John 1:1-18. The Easter Liturgy Gospel Reading in the Orthodox Church.)

Jesus, the divine Word of God in human flesn, comes to teach men by his presence, his words and his deeds. His disciples are sent into the world to proclaim Him and His **Gospel**, which means literally the "glad tidings" or the "good news" of the Kingdom of God. Those whom Jesus sends are called the **apostles**, which means literally "those who are sent." The apostles are directly inspired by God's Holy Spirit, the Spirit of Truth (John 15:26), to **"make disciples of all nations"** teaching them what Christ has commanded. (Matthew 28:19)

The early Church, we are told, **"devoted themselves to the apostles' doctrine." (Acts 2:42) Doctrine** as a word simply means teaching or instruction. The apostles' doctrine is the doctrine of Jesus and becomes the doctrine of the Christian Church. It is received by the disciples of every age and generation as the very doctrine of God. It is proclaimed everywhere and always as the doctrine of eternal life through which all men and the whole world are enlightened and saved.

At this point it must be mentioned that although God's self-revelation in history through the chosen people of Israel—the revelation which culminates in the coming of Christ the Messiah--is of primary importance, it is also the doctrine of the Christian Church that all genuine strivings of men after the truth are fulfilled in Christ. Every genuine insight into the meaning of life finds its perfection in the Christian Gospel. Thus, the holy fathers of the Church taught that the yearnings of pagan religions and the wisdom of many philosophers are also capable of serving to prepare men for the doctrines of Jesus and are indeed valid and genuine ways to the one Truth of God.

10

In this way Christians considered certain Greek philosophers to have been enlightened by God to serve the cause of Truth and to lead men to fullness of life in God since the Word and Wisdom of God is revealed to all men and is found in all men who in the purity of their minds and hearts have been inspired by the Divine Light which enlightens every man who comes into this world. This Divine Light is the word of God, Jesus of Nazareth in human flesh, the perfection and fullness of God's self-revelation to the world.

It cannot be overstressed that divine revelation in the Old Testament, in the Church of the New Testament, in the lives of the saints, in the wisdom of the fathers, in the beauty of creation . . . and most fully and perfectly in Jesus Christ, the Son of God, is the revelation of God Himself. God has spoken. God has acted. God has manifested Himself and continues to manifest Himself in the lives of His people.

If we want to hear God's voice and see God's actions of self-revelation in the world, we must purify our minds and hearts from everything that is wicked and false. We must strive to love the truth, to love one another, and to love everything in God's good creation. According to the Orthodox faith, purification from falsehood and sin is the way to the knowledge of God. If we open ourselves to divine grace and purify ourselves from all evils, then it is certain that we will be able to interpret the scriptures properly and come into living communion with the true and living God who has revealed Himself and continues to reveal Himself to those who love Him.

Tradition

The ongoing life of God's People is called **Holy Tradition**. The Holy Tradition of the Old Testament is expressed in the Old Testamental part of the Bible and in the ongoing life of the People of Israel until the birth of Christ. This tradition is fulfilled, completed and transcended in the time of the Messiah and in the Christian Church.

The New Testamental or Christian Tradition is also called the **apostolic tradition** and the **tradition of the Church**. The central written part of this tradition is the New Testamental writings in the Bible. The gospels and the other writings of the apostolic church form the heart of the Christian tradition and are the main written source and inspiration of all that developed in later ages.

This Christian tradition is given over from people to people, through space and time. **Tradition** as a word means exactly this: it is that which is "passed on" and "given over" from one to another. **Holy Tradition** is, therefore, that which is passed on and given over within the Church from the time of Christ's apostles right down to the present day.

Although containing many written documents, Holy Tradition is not at all limited to what is written; it is not merely a body of literature. It is, on the contrary, the total life and experience of the entire Church transferred from place to place and from generation to generation. **Tradition** is the very life of the Church itself as it is inspired and guided by the Holy Spirit.

Not everything in the Church belongs to its Holy Tradition for not everything in the Church is done by the grace of the Holy Spirit, and not everything in the Church pertains essentially and necessarily to the Kingdom of God. Some things in the Church are just temporal and temporary things, merely human customs and traditions of no eternal and everlasting value. Such things in themselves are not sinful or wrong. On the contrary, they may be very positive and very helpful to the life of the Church as long as they are not taken to be what they are not. Thus, it is very important in the Church to make the distinction between traditions which are merely earthly and human and passing away and the genuine Holy Tradition which pertains to the heavenly and eternal Kingdom of God.

It is also important to recognize that there are also things in the Church which not only do not belong to Holy Tradition, but which are not even to be counted among its positive human traditions. These things which are just sinful and wrong are brought into the life of the Church from the evil world. The Church in its human form, as an earthly institution, is not immune to the sins of its unholy members. These deviations and errors which creep into the life of the Church stand under the judgment and condemnation of the authentic and genuine Holy Tradition which comes from God.

Among the elements which make up the Holy Tradition of the Church, the Bible holds the first place. Next comes the Church's liturgical life and its prayer, then its dogmatic decisions and the acts of its approved churchly councils, the writings of the church fathers, the lives of the saints, the canon laws, and finally the iconographic tradition together with the other inspired forms of creative artistic expression such as music and architecture.

All of the elements of Holy Tradition are organically linked together in real life. None of them stands alone. None may be separated or isolated from the other or from the wholeness of the life of the Church. All come alive in the actual living of the life of the Church in every age and generation, in every time and place. As the Church continues to live by the inspiration of the Holy Spirit, the Holy Tradition of the Church will continue to grow and develop. This process will go on until the establishment of the Kingdom of God at the end of the ages.

13

Bible

The written record of God's revelation is the **Bible**, which means the book, or the books. The Bible is also called the **Holy Scriptures. Scripture** as a word simply means writings.

The Bible was written over thousands of years by many different people. It is divided into two **testaments** or **covenants**. These words signify agreements, pacts, or we might say, "deals." The two basic covenants are the old and the new; each has its own scriptures. As a book, the Bible contains many different kinds of writings: law, prophecy, history, poetry, stories, aphorisms, prayers, letters and symbolical visions.

The Old Testament

The Old Testament scripture begins with the five books of the **Law** called the **Pentateuch**, which means the five books; also called the **Torah**, which means the Law. Sometimes these books are also called the **Books of Moses** since they are centered on the exodus and the Mosaic laws.

In the Old Testament there are also books of the history of Israel; books called the **Wisdom** books such as the Psalms, Proverbs and the Book of Job; and books of the prophecies which carry the names of the Old Testament prophets. A **prophet** is one who speaks the Word of God by direct divine inspiration. Only secondarily does the word prophet mean one who foretells the future.

The Orthodox Church also numbers among the genuine books of the Old Testament the so-called **apocryphal** books, meaning literally the secret or hidden writings. Other Christians put these books in a secondary place or reject completely their being of divine inspiration. (see chart)

14

The New Testament

The center of the New Testament part of the Bible is the four gospels of Matthew, Mark, Luke and John who are called the four **evangelists**, which means those who wrote the gospels. Gospel in Greek is **evangelion** which, as we have seen, means the "glad tidings" or the "good news."

In the New Testament scripture there is also the book of the **Acts of the Apostles**, written by St. Luke. There are fourteen letters called the **epistles** (which simply means letters) of the Apostle Paul, though perhaps some, such as the **Letter to the Hebrews**, were not written directly by him. Three letters are also ascribed to the Apostle John; two to the Apostle Peter; and one each to the Apostles James and Jude. Finally there is the **Book of Revelation**, also called the **Apocalypse**, which is ascribed to St. John as well. (see chart)

For the Orthodox, the Bible is the main written source of divine doctrine since God Himself inspired its writing by His Holy Spirit. (see II Timothy 3:16 and II Peter 1:20) This is the doctrine of the **inspiration** of the Bible, namely that men inspired by God wrote the words which are truly their own human words--all words are human!--but which nevertheless may be called all together the **Word of God**. Thus, the Bible is the Word of God in written form because it contains not merely the thoughts and experiences of men, but the very self-revelation of God.

The center of the Bible as the written Word of God in human form is the person of the Living Word of God in human form, Jesus Christ. All parts of the Bible are interpreted in the Orthodox Church in the light of Christ since everything in the Bible leads up to Christ and speaks about Him. (Luke 24:44) This fact is symbolized in the Orthodox Church by the fact that only the book of the four gospels is enthroned on the altars of our churches and not the entire Bible. This is so because everything in the Bible is fulfilled in Christ.

The Old Testament

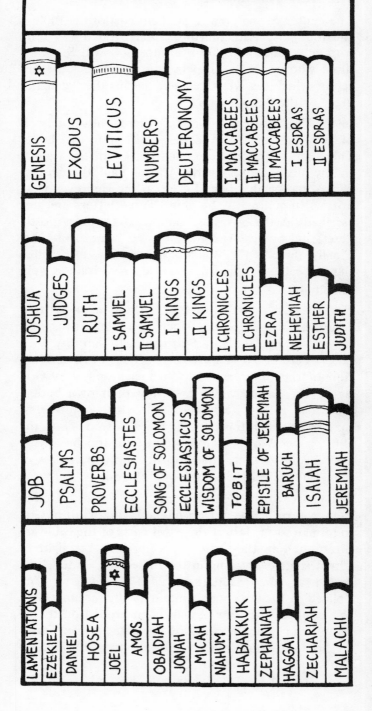

GENESIS
EXODUS
LEVITICUS
NUMBERS
DEUTERONOMY
I MACCABEES
II MACCABEES
III MACCABEES
I ESDRAS
II ESDRAS

JOSHUA
JUDGES
RUTH
I SAMUEL
II SAMUEL
I KINGS
II KINGS
I CHRONICLES
II CHRONICLES
EZRA
NEHEMIAH
ESTHER
JUDITH

JOB
PSALMS
PROVERBS
ECCLESIASTES
SONG OF SOLOMON
ECCLESIASTICUS
WISDOM OF SOLOMON
TOBIT
EPISTLE OF JEREMIAH
BARUCH
ISAIAH
JEREMIAH

LAMENTATIONS
EZEKIEL
DANIEL
HOSEA
JOEL
AMOS
OBADIAH
JONAH
MICAH
NAHUM
HABAKKUK
ZEPHANIAH
HAGGAI
ZECHARIAH
MALACHI

The New Testament

MATTHEW
MARK
LUKE
JOHN
ACTS OF THE APOSTLES

ROMANS
I CORINTHIANS
II CORINTHIANS
GALATIANS
EPHESIANS
PHILIPPIANS
COLOSSIANS
I THESSALONIANS
II THESSALONIANS
I TIMOTHY
II TIMOTHY
TITUS
PHILEMON

HEBREWS
JAMES
I PETER
II PETER

I JOHN
II JOHN
III JOHN
JUDE
REVELATION

The Liturgy

When the Church, which means literally the gathering or assembly of people who are called together to perform a specific task, assembles as God's People to worship, this gathering is called the **liturgy** of the Church. As a word **liturgy** means the common work or action of a particular group of people for the sake of all. Thus the **divine liturgy** of the Christian Church means the common work of God done by the people of God.

The liturgy of the Old Testament people was the official worship in the temple of Jerusalem according to the Mosaic Law, as well as the annual feasts and fasts and the private prayers and services held by the Israelites at home or in the synagogues. **Synagogues** by definition are houses of gathering; they are not temples since according to the Law there was just the one **temple** in Jerusalem where the priestly worship was conducted. In the synagogues the Israelites gathered for prayer and scriptural study, preaching and contemplation of the Word of God.

In the New Testament Church the liturgy is centered in the person of Christ and is primarily a "christening" of the Old Testament liturgical life. The Christian Church retains the liturgical life of the Old Testament in a new and eternal perspective. Thus, the prayers of the Old Testament, the scriptures and the psalms, are read and sung in the light of Christ. The sacrifice of the Body and Blood of Christ replaces the Old Testament sacrifices in the temple. And the Lord's Day, Sunday, replaces the old Jewish sabbath which is Saturday.

The Jewish feasts also take on new meaning in the Christian Church with the central feast of Passover, for example, becoming the celebration of Christ's death and resurrection; and the feast of Pentecost becoming the celebration of the coming of the Holy Spirit which fulfills the Old Testamental Law. The Christian liturgical year is also patterned after the Old Testamental prototype.

18

From the basic foundation of the Old Testament liturgy the Church developed its own sacramental life with baptism in the name of the Holy Trinity, chrismation, holy communion, marriage, repentance, healing and the Churchly ministry and priesthood taking on specifically Christian forms and meaning. In addition, a great wealth of specifically Christian prayers, hymns and blessings were developed, together with specifically Christian feasts and celebrations in remembrance of New Testamental events and saints.

The living experience of the Christian sacramental and liturgical life is a primary source of Christian doctrine. In the liturgy of the Church, the Bible and the Holy Tradition come alive and are given to the living experience of the Christian people. Thus, through prayer and sacramental worship men are "taught by God" as it was predicted for the messianic age. (John 6:45)

In addition to the living experience of the liturgy, the texts of the services and sacraments provide a written source of doctrine in that they may be studied and contemplated by one who desires an understanding of Christian teachings. According to the common opinion of the Orthodox Church, the sacramental and liturgical texts--the hymns, blessings, prayers, symbols, and rituals--contain no formal errors or deformations of the Christian faith and can be trusted absolutely to reveal the genuine doctrine of the Orthodox Church. It may well be that some of the historical information contained in church feasts is inaccurate or merely symbolical, but there is no question in the Church that the doctrinal and spiritual meaning of all of the feasts is genuine and authentic and provides true experience and knowledge of God.

The Councils

As the Church progressed through history it was faced with many difficult decisions. The Church always settled difficulties and made decisions by reaching a consensus of opinion among all the believers inspired by God who were led by their appointed leaders, first the apostles and then the bishops.

The first church council in history was held in the apostolic church to decide the conditions under which the gentiles, that is, the non-Jews, could enter the Christian Church. (see Acts 15) From that time on, all through history councils were held on every level of church life to make important decisions. Bishops met regularly with their priests, also called presbyters or elders, and people. It became the practice, and even the law, very early in church history that bishops in given regions should meet in councils held on a regular basis.

At times in church history councils of all of the bishops in the church were called. All the bishops were not able to attend these councils, of course, and not all such councils were automatically approved and accepted by the Church in its Holy Tradition. In the Orthodox Church only seven such councils, some of which were actually quite small in terms of the number of bishops attending, have received the universal approval of the entire Church in all times and places. These councils have been termed the **Seven Ecumenical Councils**. (see chart)

The dogmatic definitions (**dogma** means official teaching) and the canon laws of the ecumenical councils are understood to be inspired by God and to be expressive of His will for men. Thus, they are essential sources of Orthodox Christian doctrine.

Besides the seven ecumenical councils, there are other local church councils whose decisions have also received the approval of all Orthodox Churches in the world, and so are considered to be genuine expressions of the Orthodox faith and life. The decisions of these councils are mostly of a moral or structural character. Nevertheless, they too reveal the teaching of the Orthodox Church.

The Seven Ecumenical Councils

Nicea I	325	Formulated the First Part of the Creed, defining the divinity of the Son of God.
Constantinople I	381	Formulated the Second Part of the Creed, defining the divinity of the Holy Spirit.
Ephesus	431	Defined Christ as the Incarnate Word of God and Mary as Theotokos.
Chalcedon	451	Defined Christ as Perfect God and Perfect Man in One Person.
Constantinople II	553	Reconfirmed the Doctrines of the Trinity and of Christ.
Constantinople III	680	Affirmed the True Humanity of Jesus by insisting upon the reality of His human will and action.
Nicea II	787	Affirmed the propriety of icons as genuine expressions of the Christian Faith.

Fathers

There are in the Church a number of saints who were theologians and spiritual teachers who defended and explained the doctrines of the Christian Faith. These saints are called the **holy fathers** of the Church and their teachings are called the **patristic** teachings. (Patristic is from the Greek word for father.)

Some of the holy fathers are called **apologists** because they defended the Christian teachings against those outside the Church who ridiculed the faith. Their writings are called **apologies** which means "answers" or "defenses."

Others of the holy fathers defended the Christian faith against certain members of the Church who deformed the truth and life of Christianity by choosing certain parts of the Christian revelation and doctrine while denying other aspects. Those who deformed the Christian faith in this way and thereby destroyed the integrity of the Christian Church are called the heretics, and their doctrines are called heresies. By definition **heresy** means "choice," and a **heretic** is one who chooses what he wants according to his own ideas and opinions, selecting certain parts of the Christian Tradition while rejecting others. By his actions a heretic not only destroys the fullness of the Christian truth but also divides the life of the Church and causes division in the community.

Generally speaking, the Orthodox tradition regards the teachers of heresies as not merely being mistaken or ignorant or misguided; it accuses them of being actively aware of their actions and therefore sinful. A person merely misguided or mistaken or teaching what he believes to be the truth without being challenged or opposed as to his possible errors is not considered to be a heretic in the true sense of the word. Many of the saints and even the holy fathers have elements in their teachings which Christians of later times have considered as being false or inaccurate. This, of course, does not make them heretics.

Not all of the holy fathers were defenders against falsehood or heresy. Some of them were simply the very positive teachers of the Christian faith, developing and explaining its meaning in a deeper and fuller way. Others were teachers of the spiritual life, giving instruction to the faithful about the meaning and method of communion with God through prayer and Christian living. Those teachers who concentrated on the struggle of spiritual life are called the **ascetical** fathers, **asceticism** being the exercise and training of the "spiritual athletes"; and those who concentrated on the way of spiritual communion with God are called the **mystical** fathers, **mysticism** being defined as the genuine, experiential union with the Divine.

All of the holy fathers, whether they are classified as theological, pastoral, ascetical or mystical gave their teachings from the sources of their own living Christian experience. They defended and described and explained the theological doctrines and ways of spiritual life from their own living knowledge of these realities. They blended together the brilliance of the intellect with the purity of the soul and the righteousness of life. This is what makes them the holy fathers of the Church.

The writings of the Church Fathers are not infallible, and it has even been said that in any given one of them some things could be found which could be questioned in the light of the fullness of the Tradition of the Church. Nevertheless, taken as a whole, the writings of the Fathers which are built upon the biblical and liturgical foundations of Christian faith and life have great authority within the Orthodox Church and are primary sources for the discovery of the Church's doctrine.

The writings of some of those fathers who have received the universal approval and praise of the Church through the ages are of particular importance, such as those of Ignatius of Antioch, Irenaeus of Lyons,

RATTI KABEL
$ 23.50

Athanasius of Alexandria, Basil the Great, Gregory of Nyssa, Gregory the Theologian, John Chrysostom, Cyril of Alexandria, Cyril of Jerusalem, Maximus the Confessor, John of Damascus, Photius of Constantinople and Gregory Palamas: and those of the ascetical and spiritual fathers such as Anthony of Egypt, Macarius of Egypt, John of the Ladder, Isaac of Syria, Ephraim of Syria, Simeon the New Theologian and others.

Sometimes it is difficult for us to read the writings of the fathers of the Church since their problems were often complicated and their manner of writing very different in style from our own. Also most of the spiritual and ascetical writings are put in the monastic setting and have to be transposed in order to be understandable and usable to those of us who are not monks or nuns. Nevertheless, it is important to read the writings of the fathers directly. One should do so slowly, a little at a time, with careful thought and consideration and without making quick and capricious conclusions . . . the same way that one would read the Bible. Among the church fathers, Saint John Chrysostom's writings are very clear and direct and can be read by many with great profit if the proper care is given. Also the **Philokalia,** an anthology of spiritual writings, exists in English, at least in part, and with proper care, it can be helpful to a mature Christian in search of deeper insights into the spiritual life. (See Book IV on *Spirituality*)

The Saints

The doctrine of the Church comes alive in the lives of the true believers, the **saints**. The saints are those who literally share the holiness of God. **"Be holy, for I your God am holy."** (**Leviticus 11:44; I Peter 1:16**) The lives of the saints bear witness to the authenticity and truth of the Christian gospel, the sure gift of God's holiness to men.

In the Church there are different classifications of saints. In addition to the holy fathers who are quite specifically glorified for their teaching, there are a number of classifications of the various types of holy people according to the particular aspects of their holiness.

Thus, there are the **apostles** who are sent to proclaim the Christian faith, the **evangelists** who specifically announce and even write down the gospels, the **prophets** who are directly inspired to speak God's word to men. There are the **confessors** who suffer for the faith and the **martyrs** who die for it. There are the so-called **"holy ones"**, the saints from among the monks and nuns; and the **"righteous"** those from among the lay people.

In addition, the church service books have a special title for saints from among the ordained clergy and another special title for the holy rulers and statesmen. Also there is the strange classification of the **fools for Christ's sake.** These are they who through their total disregard for the things that people consider so necessary—clothes, food, money, houses, security, public reputation, etc.—have been able to witness without compromise to the Christian Gospel of the Kingdom of Heaven. They take their name from the sentence of the Apostle Paul: **"We are fools for Christ's sake.."** (**I Corinthians 4:10; 3:18**)

There are volumes on lives of the saints in the Orthodox tradition. They may be used very fruitfully for the discovery of the meaning of the Christian faith and life. In these "lives" the Christian vision of God, man, and the world stands out very clearly. Because these volumes were written down in times quite different from our own, it is necessary to read them carefully to distinguish the essential points from the artificial and sometimes even fanciful embellishments which are often contained in them. In the Middle Ages, for instance, it was customary to pattern the lives of saints after literary works of previous times and even to dress up the lives of the lesser known saints after the manner of earlier saints of the same type. It also was the custom to add many elements, particularly supernatural and miraculous events of the most extraordinary sort, to confirm the true holiness of the saint, to gain strength for his spiritual goodness and truth, and to foster imitation of his virtues in the lives of the hearers and readers. In many cases the miraculous is added to stress the ethical righteousness and innocence of the saint in the face of his detractors.

Generally speaking, it does not take much effort to distinguish the sound kernel of truth in the lives of the saints from the additions made in the spirit of piety and enthusiasm of the later periods; and the effort should be made to see the essential truth which the lives contain. Also, the fact that elements of a miraculous nature were added to the lives of saints during medieval times for the purposes of edification, entertainment and even amusement should not lead to the conclusion that all things miraculous in the lives of the saints are invented for literary or moralizing purposes. Again, a careful reading of the lives of the saints will almost always reveal what is authentic and true in the realm of the miraculous. Also, the point has been rightly made that men can learn **almost** as much about the real meaning of Christianity from the **legends** of the saints produced within the tradition of the Church as from the authentic **lives** themselves.

Canons

There are canon laws of ecumenical councils, of provincial and local councils, and of individual church fathers which have been received by the entire Orthodox Church as normative for Christian doctrine and practice. As a word **canon** means literally rule or norm or measure of judging. In this sense the canon laws are not positive laws in the juridical sense and cannot be easily identified with laws as understood and operative in human jurisprudence.

The canons of the Church are distinguished first between those of a dogmatic or doctrinal nature and those of a practical, ethical, or structural character. They are then further distinguished between those which may be changed and altered and those which are unchangeable and may not be altered under any conditions.

The dogmatic canons are those council definitions which speak about an article of the Christian faith; for example, the nature and person of Jesus Christ. Although such canons may be explained and developed in new and different words, particularly as the Church Tradition grows and moves through time, their essential meaning remains eternal and unchanging.

Some canons of a moral and ethical character also belong to those which cannot be changed. These are the moral canons whose meaning is absolute and eternal and whose violation can in no way be justified. The canons which forbid the sale of Church sacraments are of this kind.

There are, in addition, canons of a quite practical nature which may be changed and which, in fact, have been changed in the course of the life of the Church. There are also those which may be changed but which remain in force since the Church has shown the desire to retain them. An example of the former type is the canon which requires the priests of the church to be ordained to office only after reaching thirty years of age. It might be said that although this type of canon remains normative and does set a certain ideal which theoretically may still be of value, the needs of the Church have led to its violation in actual life. The canon which requires that the bishops of the Church be unmarried is of the latter type.

It is not always clear which canons express essential marks of Christian life and which do not. There are often periods of controversy over certain canons as to their applicability in given times and conditions. These factors, however, should not lead the members of the Church to dismay or to the temptation either to enforce all canons blindly with identical force and value or to dismiss all the canons as meaningless and insignificant.

In the first place, the canons are "of the Church" and therefore cannot possibly be understood as "positive laws" in a juridical sense; secondly, the canons are certainly not exhaustive, and do not cover every possible aspect of Church faith and life; thirdly, the canons were produced for the most part in response to some particular dogmatic or moral question or deviation in the Church life and so usually bear the marks of some particular controversy in history which has conditioned not merely their particular formulation, but indeed their very existence.

Taken by themselves, the canon laws of the Church can be misleading and frustrating, and therefore superficial people will say "either enforce them all or discard them completely." But taken as a whole within the wholeness of Orthodox life--theological, historical, canonical, and spiritual--these canons do assume their proper place and purpose and show themselves to be a rich source for discovering the living Truth of God in the Church. In viewing the canons of the Church the key factors are Christian knowledge and wisdom which are borne from technical study and spiritual depth. There is no other "key" to their usage; and any other way would be according to the Orthodox faith both unorthodox and unchristian.

Church Art

The Orthodox Church has a rich tradition of iconography as well as other church arts: music, architecture, sculpture, needlework, poetry, etc. This artistic
tradition is based on the Orthodox Christian doctrine
of human creativity rooted in God's love for man and
the world in creation.

Because man is created in the image and likeness of
God, and because God so loved man and the world as
to create, save and glorify them by His own coming in
Christ and the Holy Spirit, the artistic expressions of
man and the blessings and inspirations of God merge
into a holy artistic creativity which truly expresses
the deepest truths of the Christian vision of God,
man, and nature.

The **icon** is Orthodoxy's highest artistic achievement.
It is a gospel proclamation, a doctrinal teaching and a
spiritual inspiration in colors and lines.

The traditional Orthodox icon is not a holy picture.
It is not a pictorial portrayal of some Christian saint
or event in a "photocopy" way. It is, on the contrary,
the expression of the eternal and divine reality, significance, and purpose of the given person or event depicted. In the gracious freedom of the divine inspiration, the icon depicts its subject as at the same time
both human and yet "full of God," earthly and yet
heavenly, physical and yet spiritual, "bearing the
cross" and yet full of grace, light, peace and joy. In
this way the icon expresses a deeper "realism" than
that which would be shown in the simple reproduc-
tion of the physical externals of the historic person or
happening. Thus, in their own unique way the various
types of Orthodox icons, through their form and style
and manner of depiction as well as through their
actual contents and use in the Church, are an inexhaustible source of revelation of the Orthodox doctrine and faith.

Musical expression may be added to the icon as a
source of discovering the Orthodox Christian world-

view. Here, however, there is greater difficulty because of the loss in recent years of the liturgical and spiritual meaning of music in the Church. Just as the theological meaning of the traditional Orthodox icon is being rediscovered, so is the traditional doctrinal significance of Orthodox music. The process in the latter case, however, is much slower, much more difficult, and much less evident to the average person.

The traditional Orthodox architecture also expresses the doctrine of the Church, particularly in its emphasis on "God with us" and the complete communion of men and the world with God in Christ. The use of domed ceilings, the shape and layout of the buildings, the placing of the icons, the use of vestments, etc., all express the teachings of the Church. The traditional Orthodox church architecture and art work are expressions of the Orthodox Christian doctrines of creation, salvation and eternal life.

It is a very important spiritual exercise for Christians to study the holy icons and the hymns of the Church's liturgy. One can learn much about God and His gracious actions among men by a careful and prayerful contemplation of the artistic expressions of Church doctrine and life. (See Book II on *Worship*)

I AM THE WAY THE TRUTH AND THE LIFE

2

THE SYMBOL
OF FAITH

Nicene Creed

The **Nicene Creed** should be called the Nicene-Constantinopolitan Creed since it was formally drawn up at the first ecumenical council in Nicea (325) and at the second ecumenical council in Constantinople (381).

The word **creed** comes from the Latin **credo** which means "I believe." In the Orthodox Church the creed is usually called **The Symbol of Faith** which means literally the "bringing together" and the "expression" or "confession" of the faith.

In the early Church there were many different forms of the Christian confession of faith; many different "creeds." These creeds were always used originally in relation to baptism. Before being baptized a person had to state what he believed. The earliest Christian creed was probably the simple confession of faith that Jesus is the Christ, i.e. the Messiah; and that the Christ is Lord. By publicly confessing this belief, the person could be baptized into Christ, dying and rising with Him into the New Life of the Kingdom of God in the name of the Father, and of the Son, and of the Holy Spirit.

As time passed different places had different credal statements, all professing the identical faith, yet using different forms and expressions, with different degrees of detail and emphasis. These credal forms usually became more detailed and elaborate in those areas where questions about the faith had arisen and heresies had developed.

In the fourth century a great controversy developed in Christendom about the nature of the **Son of God** (also called in the Scripture the Word or Logos). Some said that the Son of God is a creature like everything else made by God. Others contended that the Son of God is eternal, divine, and uncreated. Many councils met and made many statements of faith about the nature of the Son of God. The controversy raged throughout the entire Christian world.

It was the definition of the council which the Emperor Constantine called in the city of Nicea in the year 325 which was ultimately accepted by the Orthodox Church as the proper Symbol of Faith. This council is now called the first ecumenical council, and this is what it said:

> We believe in one God, the Father Almighty, Maker of heaven and earth, and of all things visible and invisible. And in one Lord Jesus Christ, the Son of God, the only-begotten, begotten of the Father before all ages. Light of Light; true God of true God; begotten, not made; of one essence with the Father, by whom all things were made; who for us men and for our salvation came down from heaven, and was incarnate of the Holy Spirit and the Virgin Mary, and became man. And He was crucified for us under Pontius Pilate, and suffered, and was buried. And the third day He rose again, according to the Scriptures; and ascended into heaven, and sits at the right hand of the Father; and He shall come again with glory to judge the living and the dead; whose Kingdom shall have no end.

Following the controversy about the Son of God, the Divine Word, and essentially connected with it, was the dispute about the Holy Spirit. The following definition of the Council in Constantinople in 381. which has come to be known as the second ecumenical council was added to the Nicene statement:

> And (we believe) in the Holy Spirit, the Lord, the Giver of Life, who proceeds from the Father; who with the Father and the Son together is worshipped and glorified; who spoke by the prophets. In one Holy, Catholic, and Apostolic Church. I acknowledge one baptism for the remission of sins. I look for the resurrection of the dead, and the life of the world to come. Amen.

This whole Symbol of Faith was ultimately adopted throughout the entire Church. It was put into the first person form "I believe" and used for the formal and official confession of faith made by a person (or his sponsor-godparent) at his baptism. It is also used as the formal statement of faith by a non-Orthodox Christian entering the communion of the Orthodox Church. In the same way the creed became part of the life of Orthodox Christians and an essential element of the Divine Liturgy of the Orthodox Church at which each person formally and officially accepts and renews his baptism and membership in the Church. Thus, the Symbol of Faith is the only part of the liturgy (repeated in another form just before Holy Communion) which is in the first person. All other songs and prayers of the liturgy are plural, beginning with "we". Only the credal statement begins with "I." This, as we shall see, is because faith is first personal, and only then corporate and communal.

To be an Orthodox Christian is to affirm the Orthodox Christian faith, - not merely the words, but the essential meaning of the Nicene-Constantinopolitan symbol of faith. It means as well to affirm all that this statement implies, and all that has been expressly developed from it and built upon it in the history of the Orthodox Church over the centuries down to the present day.

Faith

I believe

Faith is the foundation of Christian life. It is the fundamental virtue of Abraham, the forefather of Israel and the Christian Church. **"Abraham believed the Lord, and he counted it to him as righteousness."** (Genesis 15:6)

Jesus begins his ministry with the same command for faith.

> **"...Jesus came into Galilee, preaching the gospel of God and saying, 'The time is fulfilled, the kingdom of God is at hand; repent and believe in the gospel.'"** (Mark 1:15)

All through his life Jesus was calling for faith; faith in himself, faith in God his Father, faith in the Gospel, faith in the Kingdom of God. The fundamental condition of the Christian life is faith, for with faith come hope and love and every good work and every good gift and power of the Holy Spirit. This is the doctrine of Christ, the apostles, and the Church.

In the Scriptures faith is classically defined as **"the assurance of things hoped for, the conviction of things not seen."** (Hebrews 11:1)

There are basically two aspects to faith; one might even say two meanings of faith. The first is faith "in" someone or something, faith as the recognition of these persons or things as real, true, genuine, and valuable; for example, faith in God, in Christ, in the Holy Trinity, in the Church. The second is faith in the sense of trust or reliance. In this sense, for example, one would not merely believe in God, in his existence, goodness, and truth; but one would believe God, trust his word, rely upon his presence, depend securely and with conviction upon his promises. For Christians both types of faith are necessary. One must believe in certain things with mind, heart, and soul; and then live by them in the course of everyday life.

Faith is sometimes opposed to **reason**, and belief to **knowledge**. According to Orthodoxy, faith and reason, belief and knowledge, are indeed two different things. They are two different things, however, which always belong together and which may never be opposed to each other or separated from each other.

In the first place one cannot believe anything which he does not already somehow know. A person cannot possibly believe in something he knows nothing about. Secondly, what one believes in and trusts must be reasonable. If asked to believe in the divinity of a cow, or to place one's trust in a wooden idol, one would refuse on the basis that it is not reasonable to do so. Thus, faith must have its reasons, it must be built upon knowledge, it must never be blind. Thirdly, knowledge itself is often built upon faith. One cannot come to knowledge through absolute scepticism. If anything is known at all, it is because there exists a certain faith in man's knowing possibilities and a real trust that the objects of knowledge are really "showing themselves" and that the mind and the senses are not acting decitfully. Also, in relation to almost all written words, particularly those which relate to history, the reader is called to an act of faith. He must believe that the author is telling the truth; and, therefore, he must have certain knowledge and certain reasons for giving his trust.

Very often it is only when one does give his trust and does believe something that one is able to "go further," so to speak, and to come finally to knowledge of his own and to the understanding of things he would never have understood before. It is true to say that certain things always remain obscure and meaningless unless they are viewed in the light of faith which then provides a way of explaining and understanding their existence and meaning. Thus, for example, the phenomena of suffering and death would be understood differently by one who believes in Christ than by one who believes in some other religion or philosophy or in none at all.

Faith is always personal. Each person must believe for himself. No one can believe for another. Many people may believe and trust the same things because of a unity of their knowledge, reason, experience and convictions. There can be a community of faith and a unity of faith. But this community and unity necessarily begins and rests upon the confession of personal faith.

For this reason the Symbol of Faith in the Orthodox Church—not only at baptisms and official rituals of joining the Church, but also in common prayers and in the Divine Liturgy—always remains in the first person. If **we** can pray, offer, sing, praise, ask, bless, rejoice, and commend ourselves and each other to God in the Church and **as** the Church, it is only because each one of us can say honestly, sincerely, and with prayerful conviction: "**Lord, I believe...**"—adding, as one must, the words of the man in the gospel, "**...help thou my unbelief!**" (Mark 9:24)

In order for our faith to be genuine, we must express it in everyday life. We must act according to our faith and prove it by the goodness and power of God acting in our lives. This does not mean that we "tempt God" or "put God to the test" by doing foolish and unnecessary things just for the sake of seeing if God will participate in our foolishness. But it does mean that if we live by faith in our pursuit of righteousness, we can demonstrate the fact that God will be with us, helping and guiding us in every way.

For faith to grow and become stronger, it must be used. Each person should live according to the measure of faith which he has, however small, weak and imperfect it might be. By acting according to one's faith, trust in God and the certitude of God's presence is given, and with the help of God many things which were never before imagined become possible.

God

One God, the Father Almighty

The fundamental faith of the Christian Church is in the one true and living God.

> "Hear, O Israel: the Lord our God is one God; and you shall love the Lord your God with all your heart, with all your soul and with all your might. And these words which I command you this day shall be placed upon your heart, and you shall teach them to your children, and you shall talk of them when you sit in your house, and when you walk by the way, and when you lie down and when you rise..." (Deuteronomy 6:4-8)

These words from the Law of Moses are quoted by Christ as the first and greatest commandment. (Mark 12:29) They follow upon the listing of the Ten Commandments which begin, "I am the Lord your God... you shall have no other gods besides me." (Deuteronomy 5:6-7)

The one Lord and God of Israel revealed to man the mystery of his name.

> And Moses said... "...if they ask me, 'What is his name?' what shall I say to them?"
>
> God said to Moses, "I AM WHO I AM." And he said, "Say to the people of Israel, 'I AM has sent me to you.'"
>
> God also said to Moses, "Say to the people of Israel, 'Yahweh, the God of your fathers, the God of Abraham, the God of Isaac, the God of Jacob has sent me to you: this is my name forever, and thus I am to be remembered throughout all generations.'" (Exodus 3:13-15)

God's name is **Yahweh** which means I AM WHO I AM; or I AM WHAT I AM; or I WILL BE WHAT I WILL BE; or simply I AM. He is the true and living God, the only God. He is faithful and true to his people. He reveals to them His divine and holy Word. He gives to them his divine and holy Spirit. He is called **Adonai**: the Lord; and his holy name of

Yahweh is never mentioned by the people because of its awesome sacredness. Only the high priest, and only once a year, and only in the holy of holies of the Jerusalem Temple dared to utter the divine name of Yahweh. On all other occasions **Yahweh** is addressed as the Almighty Lord, as the Most High God, as the Lord God of Hosts.

According to the Scriptures and the experience of the saints of both the old and new testaments, **Yahweh** is absolutely **holy**. This means literally that He is absolutely different and unlike anything or anyone else that exists. (**Holy** literally means totally separated, different, other.)

According to the Biblical-Orthodox tradition, even to say that "God exists" must be qualified by the affirmation that He is so unique and so perfect that His existence cannot be compared to any other. In this sense God is "above existence" or "above being." Thus, there would be great reluctance according to Orthodox doctrine to say that God "is" as everything else "is" or that God is simply the "supreme being" in the same chain of "being" as everything else that is.

In this same sense the Orthodox doctrine holds that God's unity or oneness is also not merely equivalent to the mathematical or philosophical concept of "one"; nor is his life, goodness, wisdom, and all powers and virtues ascribed to Him merely equivalent to any idea, even the greatest idea, which man can have about such reality.

However, having warned about an overly-clear or overly-positivistic concept or idea of God, the Orthodox Church--on the basis of the living experience of God in the saints--still makes the following affirmations: God may certainly be said to exist perfectly and absolutely as the one who is perfect and absolute life, goodness, truth, love, wisdom, knowledge, unity, purity, joy, simplicity; the perfection and super-perfection of everything that man knows as holy, true,

and good. It is this very God who is confessed formally in the Liturgy of St. John Chrysostom as
"...God, ineffable, inconceivable, invisible, incomprehensible, ever-existing and eternally the same."

It is this God — the Yahweh of Israel — whom Jesus
Christ has claimed to be His Father. God Almighty is
known as "Father" through His son Jesus Christ.
Jesus taught man to call the Almighty Lord God of
Hosts by the title of Father. Before Jesus no one
dared to pray to God with the intimate name of
Father. It was Jesus who said, "Pray then like this:
Our Father who art in heaven . . ."

Jesus could call God **Father** because He is God's only-
begotten Son. Christians can call God **Father** because
through Christ they receive the Holy Spirit and become themselves sons of God.

> **For when the time had fully come, God sent
> forth His Son, born of woman, born under the
> Law, to redeem those under the law, so that we
> might receive adoption as sons** (or, so that we all
> might be made sons). **And because you are sons,
> God has sent the Spirit of His Son into our hearts,
> crying "Abba! Father!" So through God you are
> no longer a slave but a son, and if a son then an
> heir** (of the Kingdom of God). **(Galatians 4:4-7;
> The Christmas Epistle Reading in the Orthodox
> Church)**

Thus no man is naturally a son of God and no man
can easily call God Father. We can only do so because
of Christ and the gift of the Holy Spirit. And so we
say in the Orthodox Divine Liturgy:

> **And make us worthy, O Master, that with bold-
> ness and without condemnation, we may dare to
> call upon Thee, the Heavenly God as Father and
> to say: Our Father, who art in heaven...**

In contemplating the revelation of God our Father in
the life of His people in the Old Testament and in the

life of the Church in the New Testament, certain attributes and properties of God can be grasped by men. First of all, it can be clearly seen that God is Love, and that in all of His actions in and toward the world, God the Father expresses His nature as Love through Christ and the Holy Spirit.

> Beloved, let us love one another; for love is of God, and he who loves is born of God and knows God. He who does not love does not know God; for God is love.

> In this the love of God was made manifest among us, that God sent His only-begotten Son into the world, so that we might live through Him. In this is love, not that we loved God, but that He loved us, and sent His Son to be the expiation for our sins.

> So we know and believe that love God has for us. God is love, and he who abides in love abides in God, and God abides in him. (1 John 4:7-16)

> . . . God's love has been poured into our hearts through the Holy Spirit which has been given to us. (Romans 5:5)

Being the God who is Love, our Father in heaven does all that He can for the life and salvation of man and the world. He does this because He is merciful and kind, longsuffering and compassionate, willing to forgive and to pardon man's sins so that man might share in the life and love of God. These gracious attributes of God are recalled in the scriptural psalmody normally chanted at the beginning of the divine liturgy in the Church.

> Bless the Lord, O my soul! And forget not all His benefits! Who forgives all your iniquity, who heals all your diseases! The Lord is compassionate and merciful, longsuffering and of great goodness! (Psalm 103)

Creation

Maker of Heaven and Earth

The Orthodox Church believes that God the Father is the "**Creator** of Heaven and earth and of all things visible and invisible."

To **create** means to make out of nothing; to bring into existence that which before did not exist; or, to quote the Liturgy of St. John Chrysostom once more: "**to bring from non-existence into being.**"

The Orthodox doctrine of **creation** is that God has brought everything and everyone which exists from non-existence into being. The Scriptural description of creation is given primarily in the first chapter of **Genesis**. The main doctrinal point about creation is that God alone is uncreated and ever-existing. Everything which exists besides God was created by Him. God, however, did not create everything individually and all at once, so to speak. He created the first foundations of existence, and then over periods of time (Perhaps millions of years--see II Peter 3:8) this first foundation of existence--by the power which God had given to it--brought forth the other creatures of God:

> Let the earth put forth vegetation....let the waters bring forth swarms of living creatures... let the earth bring forth living creatures according to their kinds..." (Genesis 1:19, 20, 24)

Thus, although God is certainly the creator of everything. He acts gradually in time and by means of things previously made by Him to which He has given life-producing potencies and powers.

According to the Orthodox Faith, everything that God makes is "very good": the heavens, the earth, the plants, the animals, and finally man himself. (Genesis 1:31) God is pleased with creation and has made it for no other purpose than to participate in His own divine, uncreated existence and to live by His own divine "**breath of life.**" **(Genesis 1:30; 2:7)**

ĪC · THE CR · EATOR · XC

By the Word of the Lord
the heavens were made,
and all their host by the
breath (or Spirit) of His mouth.

He gathered the waters of the sea as in a bottle;
He put the deeps in storehouses.

Let all the earth fear the Lord,
let all the inhabitants of the world
stand in awe of Him!
For He spoke, and it came to be!
He commanded, and it was made! (Psalm 33:6-9)

In the above-quoted verses as well as in the account of **Genesis** we must notice the presence and action of God's Word and God's Spirit. God the Father makes all that exists by means of His Divine Word—"**for He spoke and it came to be**"—and by His Divine Spirit who "**moved upon the face of the waters.**" (Genesis 1:2) We see already a glimpse of the Holy Trinity to be fully revealed in the New Testament when the Word becomes flesh and when the Holy Spirit comes personally to the disciples of Jesus on the day of Pentecost.

We must make special notice as well of the goodness of the created physical world. There is no **dualism** in Orthodox Christianity. There is no teaching that "spirit" is good and "matter" is bad, that "heaven" is good and the "earth" is evil. God loves His entire material creation with His eternal love and, as we shall see, when the physical creation is ruined by sin He does everything in His power to save it.

Loving the whole of His good creation, God the Father dwells within the world that He has made because of His goodness and love for man. The **omnipresence** of God is one of the divine attributes of the Creator particularly stressed in Orthodox Christian teaching. This fact is directly affirmed in the prayer to the Spirit of God which is used as the opening prayer of Orthodox worship:

46

O Heavenly King, the Comforter, the Spirit of
Truth, who art everywhere and fillest all things.
Treasury of Blessings and Giver of Life! Come
and abide in us. And cleanse us from every im-
purity. And save our souls, O Good One!

The fact that Christians pray: Our Father who art in
heaven . . . (or literally: **in the heavens**) is also an
affirmation of the fact that God is present everywhere, for wherever men move on the face of the
earth, over the seas or in the air, the heavens surround
them with the presence of God. The Lord Jesus
Christ, in order to have men realize that the true God,
His Father, is not bound to one or another particular
place, as were the pagan gods, teaches men to pray to
the Father "in the heavens." For the one true and
living God is present to all, over all, embracing and
encompassing all with His heavenly care and protec-
tion. The God who is "over all" is also **"through all
and in all." (Ephesians 4:5)** By His Word and His
Holy Spirit, God **"fills all in all." (Ephesians 1:10, 23)**

Thus, the Apostle Paul also proclaimed to the Atheni-
ans, that whether men realize it or not, **"in Him we
live and move and have our being,"** for **"He is not far
from each one of us." (Acts 17:27-28)** It is this fact
of God's omnipresence in His creation, and our own
presence in and to Him, that is witnessed to so
beautifully in Psalm 139:

Whither shall I go from Thy Spirit?
Or whither shall I flee from Thy Presence?
If I ascend to heaven, Thou art there!
If I make my bed in Sheol, Thou art there!
If I take the wings of the morning and dwell in the
uttermost parts of the sea, even there Thy hand
shall lead me, and Thy right hand shall hold me.
If I say, "Let only darkness cover me, and the
light about me be night," even the darkness is not
dark to Thee, the night is bright as the day; for
darkness is as light with Thee! (Psalm 139:7-12)

47

Angels

All things visible and invisible

In addition to the visible, physical creation there is an invisible world created by God. The Bible sometimes calls it "the heavens" and other times refers to it as "above the heavens." Whatever its symbolical description in the Holy Scriptures, the invisible world is definitely not part of the physical, material universe. It does not exist in space; it has no physical dimensions. And so it cannot be located, and it has no "place" which can be "reached" by travel within the galaxies of the spatial, locatable "places" of the physically created universe.

However, the fact that the invisible, created world is purely spiritual and is not discoverable on a map of the created material spaces makes it no less real or truly existing. The invisible creation exists as different from the created material universe and, of course, as totally different from the uncreated, absolutely super-divine existence of the uncreated God.

Invisible created reality consists of the **hosts of bodiless powers**, generally—and somewhat incorrectly—called the angels.

Angels (which means literally "messengers") are, strictly speaking, but one rank of the **incorporeal or bodiless powers** of the invisible world.

According to Orthodox Scripture and Tradition there are nine ranks of bodiless powers or the **Hosts** (**Sabaoth** means literally "armies" or "choirs" or "ranks.") There are **angels**, **archangels**, **principalities**, **powers**, **virtues**, **dominions**, **thrones**, **cherubim**, and **seraphim**. The latter are described as offering continual adoration and glory to God with the incessant and ever-resounding cry of Holy! Holy! Holy! (Isaiah 6:3; Revelation 4:8) Those in the middle of the above listing are little-known to men while the angels and archangels are seen as the active workers, warriors and messengers of Yahweh relative to this world. Thus, angels and archangels are seen to struggle against spiritual evil and to mediate between God and the

48

Evil Spirits

world. They appear in various forms to men in both the Old and New Testaments as well as in the life of the Church. The angels are those who bring the power and presence of God and who are messengers of His word for the salvation of the world. The best-known of the angels are Gabriel (which means literally "man of God"), the bearer of the good news of Christ's birth (Daniel 8:16; 9:21; Luke 1:19, 26), and Michael (which means literally "who is like God"), the chief warrior of the spiritual armies of God (Daniel 11:13; 12:1; Jude:9; Revelation 12:7).

Generally speaking the appearances of the bodiless powers to men are described in a physical way ("six-winged, many-eyed"; or in the "form of a man"). However, it must be clearly understood that these are merely symbolical descriptions. By nature and definition the angels have no bodies and no material properties of any sort. They are strictly spiritual beings.

Evil Spirits

In addition to the created spiritual powers who do the will of God, there are, according to the Orthodox faith, those who rebel against Him and do evil. These are the demons or **devils** (which means literally those who "pull apart" and destroy) who are also known both in the Old and New Testaments as well as in the lives of the saints of the Church.

Satan (which means literally the **enemy** or the **adversary**) is one proper name for the devil, the leader of the evil spirits. He is identified in the serpent symbol of Genesis 3 and as the tempter of both Job and Jesus. (Job 1:6; Mark 1:33) He is labelled by Christ as a deceiver and liar, the **"father of lies"** (John 8:44) and the **"prince of this world."** (John 12:31; 14:30; 16:11) He has **"fallen from heaven"** together with his evil angels to do battle with God and his servants. (Luke 10:18; Isaiah 14:12) It is this same Satan who **"entered Judas"** to effect the betrayal and destruction of Christ. (Luke 22.3)

The apostles of Christ and the saints of the Church knew from direct experience Satan's powers against man for Man's own destruction. They knew as well Satan's lack of power and his own ultimate destruction when man is with God, filled with the Holy Spirit of Christ. According to Orthodox doctrine there is no middle road between God and Satan. Ultimately, and at any given moment, man is either with God or the devil, serving one or the other.

The ultimate victory belongs to God and to those with Him. Satan and his hosts are finally destroyed. Without this recognition — and still more — the experience of this reality of the cosmic spiritual struggle (God and Satan, the good angels and the evil angels), one cannot truly be called an Orthodox Christian who sees and lives according to the deepest realities of life. Once again, however, it must be clearly noted that the devil is not a "red-suited gentlemen" nor any other type of grossly-physical tempter. He is a subtle, intelligent spirit who acts mostly by deceit and hidden actions, having as his greatest victory man's disbelief in his existence and power. Thus, the devil attacks "head-on" only those whom he can deceive in no other way: Jesus and the greatest of the saints. For the greatest part of his warfare he is only too satisfied to remain concealed and to act by indirect methods and means.

> Be sober, be watchful. Your adversary, the devil, prowls around like a roaring lion seeking someone to devour. (1 Peter 5:8)

> Put on the whole armor of God, that you may be able to stand against the wiles of the devil. For we are not contending against flesh and blood, but against the principalities, against the powers, against the world rulers of this present darkness, against the spiritual hosts of wickedness in the heavenly places. (Ephesians 6:11-12)

Man

Man is God's special creature. He is the only one "**created in the image and likeness of God.**" **(Genesis 1:26)** He is created by God from the dust at the end of the process of creation (the "sixth day") and by the special will of God. He is made to breathe "**the breath of life**" **(Genesis 2:7)**, to know God, to have dominion over all that God has made.

Man is created as di-sexual—"**male and female He created them**" **(Genesis 1:27; 2:21)**—in order "**to be fruitful and multiply.**" **(Genesis 1:28)** Thus, according to Orthodox doctrine sexuality belongs to the creation which God calls "**very good**" **(Genesis 1:31)**, and in itself it is in no way sinful or perverse. It belongs to the very nature of humanity directly willed by God.

As the image of God, ruler over creation and co-creator with the Uncreated Maker, man has the task to "reflect" God in creation; to make His presence, His will and His powers spread throughout the universe; to transform all that exists into the paradise of God. In this sense man is definitely created for a destiny higher than the bodiless powers of heaven, the angels. This conviction is affirmed by Orthodox Christianity not only because of the Scriptural emphasis on man as made in God's image to rule creation, which is not said about angels; but it is also directly affirmed because it is written of Jesus Christ, who is truly the perfect man and the Last Adam (I Corinthians 15:45) that "**God has highly exalted him and bestowed upon him the name which is above every name, that at the name of Jesus every knee should bow, in heaven and on earth and under the earth, and every tongue should confess that Jesus Christ is Lord, to the glory of God the Father.**" **(Philippians 2:10-11)**

It follows from belief in Jesus that man is created for a life far superior to that of any creature, even the angels who glorify God and serve the cause of man's salvation. It is precisely this conviction which is af-

firmed when the Church hails Mary the Mother of Christ as "more honorable than the cherubim and beyond compare more glorious than the seraphim." For what is glorified as already accomplished in the human Mary is precisely what is expected and hoped for by all men **"who hear the word of God and keep it." (Luke 11:28)**

Thus we see the great dignity of man according to the Christian faith. We see man as the "most important" of God's creatures, the one for whom "all things visible and invisible" have been created by God.

It is the Orthodox doctrine that one can understand and appreciate what it means to be human only in the light of the full revelation of Jesus Christ. Being the Divine Word and Son of God in human flesh, Jesus reveals the real meaning of manhood. As the Perfect Man and the Last Adam, the "man from heaven," Jesus gives us the proper interpretation of the story of creation given in the book of Genesis. For as the Apostle Paul has written, Adam finds his significance as **"the type (or figure) of the one who was to come,"** namely Jesus Christ. (Romans 5:14)

> **Thus it is written, "The first man Adam became a living being"; the last Adam became a life-giving spirit. But it is not the spiritual which is first but the physical, and then the spiritual. The first man was from the earth, a man of dust; the second man (Christ) is from heaven...Just as we have borne the image of the man of dust, we shall also bear the image of the man of heaven. (I Corinthians 15:45-49)**

According to Orthodox theology, to bear the image of God is to be like Christ, the uncreated Image of God, and to share in all of the spiritual attributes of divinity. It is, in the words of the holy fathers, to become by divine grace all that God Himself is by nature. If God is a free, spiritual, personal Being, so human beings, male and female, are to be the same. If God is so

powerful and creative, having dominion over all creation, so human creatures, made in His image and according to His likeness, are also to exercise dominion
in the world. If God exercises dominion and authority
not by tyranny and oppression, but by loving kindness and service, so are His creatures to do likewise.
If God Himself is love, mercy, compassion and care in
all things, so must His creatures, made to be like Him,
also be the same. And finally, if God lives forever in
eternal life, never dying, but always existing in perfectly joyful and harmonious beauty and happiness
with all of creation, so too are human beings made for
everlasting life in joyful and harmonious communion
with God and the whole of creation.

According to Orthodox doctrine, human being and
life is never completed and finished in its development
and growth because it is made in the image and according to the likeness of God. God's being and life
are inexhaustible and boundless. As the Divine Archetype has no limits to His divinity, so the human image
has no limits to its humanity, to what it can become
by the grace of its Creator. Human nature, therefore,
is created by God to grow and develop through participation in the nature of God for all eternity. Man
is made to become ever more Godlike forever, even
in the Kingdom of God at the end of this age, when
Christ will come again in glory to raise the dead and
give life to those who love Him.

Thus the holy fathers of the Orthodox faith taught
that whatever stage of maturity and development
man attains and achieves, whatever his power, wisdom, mercy, knowledge, love, there continually remains before him an infinity of ever-greater fullness
of life in the most blessed Trinity to be participated
in and lived. The fact that human nature progresses
eternally in perfection within the nature of God
constitutes the meaning of life for man, and remains
forever the source of his joy and gladness for all
eternity.

It must be mentioned at this point as well that according to Orthodox Christian doctrine, the fact that humans are created male and female is the direct will of God and is essential for proper human life and activity as reflective of God. In a word, human sexuality is a necessary element in human being and life as made in the image of God. This does not mean that there is any sort of sexuality in God, but it does mean that human life must be sexual — male and female — if it will be what God Himself has made it to be.

Man and woman, male and female, are created by God to live together in a union of being, life and love. The man is to be the leader in human activities, the one reflecting Christ as the new and perfect Adam. The woman is to be man's **"helpmeet,"** the **"mother of all living" (Genesis 2:18; 3:20)** Symbolized in the relationship of Mary and the Church, the New Eve, to Christ, the New Adam, as the one who inspires man's life and completes his being and fulfills his life, the woman is not man's instrument or tool. She is a person in her own right, a sharer of the nature of God, a necessary complement to man. There can be no man without woman — no Adam without Eve; just as there can be no woman without man. The two exist together in perfect communion and harmony for the fulfillment of human nature and life.

The differences between men and women are real and irreducible. They are not limited to biological or physical differences. They are rather different "modes of existence" within one and the same humanity; just as, we might say, the Son and the Holy Spirit are different "modes of existence" within one and the same divinity, together with God the Father. The male and female are to be in spiritual as well as bodily union. They are to express together, in one and the same humanity, all of the virtues and powers that belong to human nature as made in the image and according to the likeness of God. There are no virtues or powers that belong to man, and not to woman; nor to woman and not to man. All are called to spiritual perfection in truth and in love, indeed in all of the divine virtues of God given to His creatures.

The hostilities and competitions between man and woman that exist in the present world are not due to their respective "modes of existence" as created by God. They are due rather to sin. There should be no tyranny of men over women; no oppression, no servitude. Just as there should be no striving of women to be men, and to hold the male position in the order of creation. There should be rather a harmony and unity within the community of being with its natural created order and distinctions. The oneness of nature with the distinction of various modes of being within Divinity, the Most Holy Trinity. For in the Divinity of the Trinity Itself there is a perfect unity of nature and being, with real distinctions between the Father and the Son and the Holy Spirit as to how each of the Divine Persons lives and expresses the common nature of God. There is an **order** in the Trinity. There is even a **hierarchy** if we do not take this term to mean some difference in nature between the Father, Son and Holy Spirit, but merely the **way** in which the Divine Persons relate to One Another and to man and the world. For in the Trinity Itself the Father Alone is the "Source of divinity." The Son is the expression of the Father and is "subject" to Him. And the Holy Spirit, of one essence and fully equal with the Father and the Son, is the "third" Person who fulfills the will of the Father and the Son. The Three Divine Persons are perfectly equal. This is a dogma of the Church. But they are not the same, and there is an ordered relation between them in which there are "priorities" in being and acting which not only do not destroy the perfection and perfect unity of the Godhead, but even allow it and make it to be perfect and divine. (See Chapter III) It is the Trinitarian Life of God which is the Divine Archetype and Pattern for the being and acting of male and female within the order of creation.

Sin

The word **sin** means literally "missing the mark." It means the failure to be what one should be and to do what one should do.

Originally man was made to be the created image of God, to live in union with God's divine life, and to rule over all creation. Man's failure in this task is his sin which has also been called his **fall**.

The "fall" of man means that man failed in his God-given vocation. This is the meaning of Genesis 3. Man was seduced by evil (the serpent) into believing that he could be "like God" by his own will and effort.

In the Orthodox tradition the eating of the "tree of the knowledge of good and evil" is generally interpreted as man's actual taste of evil, his literal experience of evil as such. Sometimes, this eating is also interpreted (as by St. Gregory the Theologian) as man's attempt to go beyond what was possible for him; his attempt to do that which was not yet within his power to realize.

Whatever the details of the various interpretations of the Genesis story, it is the clear doctrine of Orthodoxy that man has failed in his original vocation. He disobeyed God's command through pride, jealousy and the lack of humble gratitude to God by yielding to the temptation of Satan. Thus man sinned. He "missed the mark" of his calling. He transgressed the Law of God (see I John 3:4). And so he ruined both himself and the creation which he was given to care for and to cultivate. By his sin—and his sins--man brings himself and all creation under the rule of evil and death.

In the Bible and in Orthodox theology these elements always go together: sin, evil, the devil, suffering and death. There is never one without the other, and all are the common result of man's rebellion against God and his loss of communion with Him. This is the primary meaning of Genesis 3 and the chapters which follow until the calling of Abraham. Sin begets still

more sin and even greater evil. It brings cosmic dis-
harmony, the ultimate corruption and death of everyone and everything. Man still remains the created
image of God—this cannot be changed—but he fails to
keep his image pure and to retain the divine likeness.
He defiles his humanity with evil, perverts it and de-
forms it so that it cannot be the pure reflection of
God that it was meant to be. The world also remains
good, indeed "very good," but it shares the sorry con-
sequences of its created master's sin and suffers with
him in mortal agony and corruption. Thus, through
man's sin the whole world falls under the rule of
Satan and **"lies in wickedness."** (I John 5:19; see also
Romans 5:12)

The Genesis story is the divinely-inspired description
in symbolic terms of man's primordial and original
possibilities and failures. It reveals that man's potency
for eternal growth and development in God was
turned instead into man's multiplication and cultiva-
tion of wickedness and his transformation of creation
into the devil's princedom, a cosmic cemetery **"groan-
ing in travail"** until saved once more by God. (Romans
8:19-23) All the children of Adam, i.e. all who belong
to the human race, share in this tragic fate. Even those
born this very minute as images of God into a world
essentially good are thrown immediately into a death-
bound universe, ruled by the devil and filled with the
wicked fruit of generations of his evil servants.

This is the fundamental message: man and the world
need to be saved. God gives the promise of salvation
from the very beginning, the promise which begins to
be fulfilled in history in the person of Abraham, the
father of Israel, the forefather of Christ.

> **And the Lord said...to Abram (later named Abra-
> ham) "I will make you a great nation...and by
> you all the families of the earth will be blessed.
> (Genesis 12:3; also 22:15)**

Abraham believed God; and from him came the people of Israel from whom, according to the flesh, came Jesus Christ the Saviour and Lord of Creation. (See Luke 1:55, 73; Romans 4; Galations 3)

The entire history of the Old Testament finds its fulfillment in Jesus. All that happened to the chosen children of Abraham happened in view of the eventual and final destruction of sin and death by Christ. The covenants of God with Abraham, Isaac and Jacob (whose name was changed to **Israel** which means "the one who struggles with God); the twelve tribes of Israel; the story of Joseph; the passover, exodus and reception of God's Law by Moses; the entrance into the promised land by Joshua; the founding of Jerusalem and the building of the temple by David and Solomon; the judges, kings, prophets and priests; everything in the Old Testament history of God's chosen people finds its final purpose and meaning in the birth, life, death, resurrection, ascension and glorification of God's only Son Jesus the Messiah. He is the one who comes from the Father to save the people from their sins, to open their tombs and to grant eternal life to all creation.

Jesus Christ

And in One Lord Jesus Christ

The fundamental confession of Christians about their
Master is this: **Jesus Christ is Lord.** It begins in the
gospel when Jesus himself asks his disciples who they
think that He is:

> **But who do you say that I am? Simon Peter re-
> plied, "You are the Christ, the Son of the Living
> God." (Matthew 16:16)**

Jesus is the Christ. This is the first act of faith which
men must make about Him. At His birth, the child of
Mary is given the name **Jesus,** which means literally
Saviour (in Hebrew **Joshua,** the name also of Moses'
successor who crossed the Jordan River and led the
chosen people into the promised land). **"You will call
his name Jesus, for he will save his people from their
sins." (Matthew 1:21; Luke 1:31)** It is this Jesus who
is the **Christ,** which means the **Anointed,** the **Messiah**
of Israel. Jesus is the Messiah, the one promised to the
world through Abraham and his children.

But who is the Messiah? This is the second question,
one also asked by Christ in the gospels--this time not
to his disciples, but to those who were taunting him
and trying to catch him in his words. "Who is the
Messiah?" he asked them, not because they could
answer or really wished to know, but in order to
silence them and to begin the inauguration of "the
hour" for which he had come: the hour of the world's
salvation.

> **Now while the Pharisees were gathered together,
> Jesus asked them a question saying, "What do
> you think of the Christ (i.e. the Messiah)? Whose
> Son is he?**
>
> **They said to him, "The Son of David."**
>
> **He said to them, "How is it then that David, in-
> spired by the Spirit, calls him Lord, saying 'The
> Lord said to my Lord, sit at my right hand till I
> put thy enemies under thy feet!'? (Psalm 110)
> If David thus calls him Lord, how is he his son?"**

And no one was able to answer him a word, nor from that day did anyone dare to ask him any more questions. (Matthew 22:41-46)

After Jesus' resurrection, inspired by the same Holy Spirit who inspired David, the apostles and all members of the Church understood the meaning of his words. Jesus is the Christ. And the Christ is the Lord. This is the mystery of Jesus Christ the Messiah, namely that He is the One and Only Lord, identified with the God Yahweh of the Old Testament.

We saw already how Yahweh was always called Adonai, the Lord, by the people of Israel. In the Greek Bible the very word Yahweh was not even written. Instead, where the word Yahweh was written in Hebrew, and where the Jews said Adonai, the Lord, the Greek Bible simply wrote **Kyrios–the Lord.** Thus, the Son of David, which was another way of saying the Messiah, is called **Kyrios**, the Lord.

For the Jews, and indeed for the first Christians, the term **Lord** was proper to God alone: **"God is the Lord and has revealed Himself unto us."** (Psalm 118) This Lord and God is Yahweh; and it is Jesus the Messiah as well. For although Jesus claims that **"the Father is greater than I"** (John 14:28), he claims as well: **"I and the Father are one."** (John 10:30)

Believing in "One Lord Jesus Christ" is the prime confession of faith for which the first Christians were willing to die. For it is the confession which claims the identity of Jesus with the Most High God.

Son of God

...the only-begotten Son of God...

Jesus is one with God as His only-begotten Son. This is the gospel proclamation formulated by the holy fathers of the Nicene Council in the following way:

> ...and in one Lord Jesus Christ, the only-begotten Son of God, begotten of the Father before all ages: Light of Light. True God of True God. Begotten not made. Of one essence with the Father. Through whom all things were made...

These lines speak about the **Son of God**, also called the **Word** or **Logos** of God, before his birth in human flesh from the Virgin Mary in Bethlehem.

There is but one eternal Son of God. He is called the **Only-begotten**, which means the only one born of God the Father. **Begotten** as a word simply means born or generated.

The Son of God is born from the Father "before all ages"; that is, before creation, before the commencement of time. Time has its beginning in creation. God exists before time, in an eternally timeless existence without beginning or end.

Eternity as a word does not mean endless time. It means the condition of no time at all—no past or future, just a constant present. For God there is no past or future. For God, all is **now**.

In the eternal "now" of God, before the creation of the world, God the Father gave birth to his only-begotten Son in what can only be termed an eternal, timeless, always presently-existing generation. This means that although the Son is "begotten of the Father" and comes forth from the Father, his coming forth is eternal. Thus, there never was a "time" when there was no Son of God. This is specifically what the heretic Arius taught. It is the doctrine formally condemned by the first ecumentical council.

Although born of the Father and having his origin in Him, the only-begotten Son always existed, or rather more accurately always "exists" as uncreated, eternal and divine. Thus, the Gospel of St. John says:

> In the beginning was the Word (the Logos-Son),
> and the Word was with God, and the Word was
> God. (John 1:1)

As the eternally-born of God and always existing with
the Father in the "timeless generation," the Son is
turly "Light of Light, True God of True God." For
God is Light and what is born of Him must be Light.
And God is True God, and what is born of Him must
be True God.

We know from the created order of things that what
is born must be essentially the same as what gives
birth. If one comes from the very being of another,
one must be the very same thing. He cannot be
essentially different. Thus, men give birth to men,
and birds to birds, fish to fish, flowers to flowers.

If God, then, in the super-abundant fullness and perfection of His divine being gives birth to a Son, the
Son must be the same as the Father in all things–
except, of course, in the fact of his being the Son.

Thus, if the Father is divinely and eternally perfect,
true, wise, good, loving, and all of the things that we
know God is: "ineffable, inconceivable, invisible, ever-
existing and eternally the same" (to quote this text of
the Liturgy once more), then the Son must be all of
these things as well. To think that what is born of
God must be less than God, says one saint of the
Church, is to dishonor to God.

The Son is "begotten not made, of one essence with
the Father." "Begotten not made" may also be put
"born and not created." Everything which exists besides God is created by Him: all things visible and invisible. But the Son of God is not a creature. He was
not created by God or made by Him. He was born,
begotten, generated from the very being and nature
of the Father.

It belongs to the very nature of God–to God as God–
according to divine revelation as understood by the
Orthodox, that God is an eternal Father by nature,

and that He should always have with Him his eternal, uncreated Son. It belongs to the very nature of God that He should be such a being if He is truly and perfectly divine. It belongs to God's very divine nature that He should not be eternally alone in his divinity, but that His very being as Love and Goodness should naturally "overflow itself" and "reproduce itself" in the generation of a divine Son: the "Son of His Love" as the Apostle Paul has called him. (Colossians 1:13 inaccurately translated in English.)

Thus, there is an abyss drawn between the created and the uncreated, between God and everything else which God has made out of nothing. The Son of God, born of the Father before all ages, is not created. He was not made out of nothing. He was eternally begotten from the divine being of the Father. He belongs "on the side of God."

Having been born and not made, the Son of God is what God is. The expression **of one essence** simply means this: what God the Father is, so also is the Son of God. **Essence** is from the Latin word **esse** which means **to be.** The essence of a thing answers the question **What is it?** What the Father is, the Son is. The Father is divine, the Son is divine. The Father is eternal, the Son is eternal. The Father is uncreated, the Son is uncreated. The Father is God and the Son is God. This is what men confess when they say "the only-begotten Son of God...of one essence with the Father."

Being always with the Father, the Son is also one life, one will, one power and one action with Him. Whatever the Father is, the Son is; and so whatever the Father does, the Son does as well. The original act of God outside of His divine existence is the act of creation. The Father is creator of heaven and earth, of all things visible and invisible. And in the act of creation, as we confess in the Symbol of Faith, the Son is the one **by whom all things were made.**

The Son acts in creation as the one who accomplishes the Father's will. The divine act of creation—and, indeed, every action toward the world in revelation, salvation, and glorification—is willed by the Father and accomplished by the Son (we will speak of the Holy Spirit below) in one identical divine action. Thus, we have the **Genesis** account of God creating through His divine word ("God said..."), and in the Gospel of St. John the following specific revelation:

He (the Word-Son) **was in the beginning with God** (the Father); **all things were made through (or by) him and without him was not anything made that was made." (John 1:2-3)**

This is the exact doctrine of the Apostle Paul as well.

...in him (the Son) **all things were created, in heaven and on earth, visible and invisible, whether thrones or dominions or principalities or powers—all things were created through him and for him. He is before all things and in him all things hold together. (Colossians 1:16-17)**

Thus, the eternal Son of God is confessed as the one **"by whom all things were made." (Hebrews 1:2; 2:10; Romans 11:36)**

The Symbol of Faith continues: **...Who for us men and for our salvation came down from heaven and was incarnate of the Holy Spirit and the Virgin Mary and became man...**

The divine Son of God was born in human flesh for the salvation of the world. This is the central doctrine of the Orthodox Christian Faith; the entire life of Christians is built upon this fact.

The Symbol of Faith stresses that it is "for us men and for our salvation" that the Son of God has come. This is the most critical biblical doctrine, that **"God so loved the world that He gave his only-begotten Son that whoever believes in Him should not perish but** have everlasting life." (John 3:16 quoted at each Divine Liturgy of St. John Chrysostom at the center of the eucharistic prayer.)

Because of his perfect love, God sent forth his Son into the world. God knew in the very act of creation that to have a world at all would require the incarnation of his Son in human flesh. **Incarnation** as a word means "enfleshment" in the sense of taking on the wholeness of human nature, body and soul.

And the Word became flesh and dwelt among us, full of grace and truth; we have beheld his glory, glory as the only-begotten Son of the Father. And from his fullness have we all received grace upon grace." (John 1:14-16)

...came down from heaven...

The affirmation that the Son has "come down from heaven and was incarnate" does not mean that the Son is located somewhere "up there" in the universe and then descended onto the planet earth. That He came "down from heaven" is the Biblical way of saying that the Son of God came from the totally "other" divine existence of God, outside the bounds and limits of all space and time located within the created, physical universe. In general we must remember again the symbolical character of all of our words and affirmations about God.

The affirmation that the Son came "down from heaven" also should not be interpreted in the sense that before the incarnation the Son of God was totally absent from the world. The Son was always "in the world" for the **"world was made through Him." (John 1:10)** He was always present in the world for He is personally the life and the light of man. (I John 4)

As "created in the image and likeness of God," every man--just by being a man--is already a reflection of the divine Son, who is Himself the uncreated image of God. (Colossians 1:15; Hebrews 1:3) Thus, the Son, or Word, or Image, or Radiance of God, as He is called in Scriptures, was always "in the world" by being always present in every of his "created images," not only as their creator, but also as the one whose very being all creatures are made to share and to reflect. Thus, in his incarnation, the Son comes personally to the world and becomes Himself a man. But even before the incarnation He was always in the world by the presence and power of his creative actions in his creatures, particularly in man.

In addition to this, it is also Orthodox doctrine that the manifestation of God to the saints of the Old Testament, the so-called **theophanies** (which means **divine manifestations**), were manifestations of the Father, by, through and in his Son or Logos. Thus, for example, the manifestations to Moses, Elias or Isaiah are mediated by God's divine and uncreated Son.

It is the Orthodox teaching as well that the Word of God which came to the Old Testament prophets and saints, and the very words of the Old Testament Law of Moses, which are called in Hebrew the "words" and not as we say in English, the "commandments", are also revelations of God by his Son, the divine Word. Thus, for example, we have Old Testamental witness to the revelation of God's Word, such as that of the Prophet Isaiah, in almost the same personalistic form as is found in the Christian gospel:

> **For as the rain and the snow come down from heaven, and return not thither but water the earth, making it bring forth and sprout, giving seed to the sower and bread to the eater, so shall my word be that goes forth from my mouth; it shall not return to me empty, but it shall accomplish that which I propose, and prosper in the thing for which I sent it. (Isaiah 55:10-11)**

Thus, before His personal birth of the Virgin Mary as the man Jesus, the divine Son and Word of God was in the world by His presence and action in creation, particularly in man. He was present and active; also in the theophanies to the Old Testament saints; and in the words of the law and the prophets, both oral and scriptural.

Incarnation

**...and He was incarnate of the Holy Spirit
and the Virgin Mary and became man**

The divine Son of God was born as a man from the
Virgin Mary by the power of the Holy Spirit. (Matthew 1; Luke 1) The Church teaches that the virgin
birth is the fulfillment of Old Testament prophecy
(Isaiah 7:14), and that it is as well the fulfillment of
the longings of all men for salvation which are found
in all religions and philosophies in human history.
Only God can save the world. Man alone cannot do it
because it is man himself who must be saved. Therefore, according to Orthodox doctrine, the virgin birth
is necessary not at all because of a false idolization of
virginity as such or because of a sinful repulsion to
normal human sexuality. Nor is it necessary as some
would contend to give "added weight" to the moral
teachings of Jesus. The virgin birth is understood as a
necessity because the one who is born must not be
merely a man like all others needing salvation. The
Saviour of the world cannot merely be one of the race
of Adam born of the flesh like all of the others. He
must be "not of this world" in order to save the world.

Jesus is born from the Virgin Mary because he is the
divine Son of God, the Saviour of the world. It is the
formal teaching of the Orthodox Church that Jesus is
not a "mere man" like all other men. He is indeed a
real man, a whole and perfectly complete man with a
human mind, soul and body. But he is the man which
the Son and Word of God has become. Thus, the
Church formally confesses that Mary should properly
be called **Theotokos**, which means literally "the one
who gives birth to God." For the one born of Mary is,
as the Orthodox Church sings at Christmas: "...he who
from all eternity is God."

> Today the Virgin gives birth to the Transcendent
> One, and the earth offers a cave to the Unap-
> proachable One! Angels, with shepherds, glorify
> Him! The wise men journey with the star! Since
> for our sake the eternal God was born as a little
> child! (Kontakion of the Nativity)

70

Jesus of Nazareth is God, or, more accurately, the divine Son of God in human flesh. He is a true man in every way. He was born. He grew up in obedience to his parents. He increased in wisdom and stature (Luke 2:51-52). He had a family life with "brethren" (Mark 2:31-34), who according to Orthodox doctrine were not children born of Mary who is confessed as "ever-virgin", but were either cousins or children of Joseph.

As a man Jesus experienced all normal and natural human experiences such as growth and development, ignorance and learning, hunger, thirst, fatigue, sorrow, pain, and disappointment. He also knew human temptation, suffering and death. He took these things upon himself "for us men and for our salvation."

> Since, therefore the children share in flesh and blood, he himself likewise partook of the same nature, that through death he might destroy him who has the power of death, that is, the devil, and deliver all those who through fear of death were subject to lifelong bondage. For surely it was not with angels that he is concerned but with the descendents of Abraham. Therefore he had to be made like his brethren in every respect ...to make expiation for the sins of the people. For because he himself has suffered and been tempted, he is able to help those who are tempted. (Hebrews 2:9-18)

Christ has entered the world becoming like all men in all things except sin.

> He committed no sin; no guile was found on his lips. When he was reviled, he did not revile in return; when he suffered, he did not threaten; but he trusted to him (God the Father) who judges justly. (I Peter 2:22; Hebrews 4:15)

Jesus was tempted, but he did not sin. He was perfect in every way, absolutely obedient to God the Father; speaking His words, doing His works, and accomplishing His will. As a man, Jesus fulfilled his role perfectly as the Perfect Man, the new and final Adam. He did all things that man fails to do, being in everything the most perfect human response to the divine initiative of God toward creation. In this sense, the Son of God as man "recapitulated" the life of Adam, i.e., the entire human race, bringing man and his world back to God the Father and allowing for a new beginning of life free from the power of sin, the devil and death.

As the Saviour-Messiah, Christ fulfilled as well all of the prophecies and expectations of the Old Testament, fulfilling and crowning in final and absolute perfection all that was begun in Israel for human and cosmic salvation. Thus, Christ is the fulfillment of the promise to Abraham, the completion of the Law of Moses, the fulfillment of the prophets and Himself the Final Prophet, the King and the Teacher, the one Great High Priest of Salvation and the Perfect Sacrificial Victim, the New Passover and the Bestower of the Holy Spirit upon all creation.

It is in this role as Messiah-King of Israel and Saviour of the world that Christ insisted upon His identity with God the Father and called Himself the Way, the Truth, and the Life: the Resurrection and the Life, the Light of the World, the Bread of Life, the Door to the Sheepfold, the Good Shepherd, the Heavenly Son of Man, the Son of God, and God Himself, the **I AM**. (Gospel of St. John)

Defense of the Doctrine of Incarnation

In the Orthodox Church the central fact of the Christian faith, that the Son of God has appeared on earth as a real man, born of the Virgin Mary in order to die and rise again to give life to the world, has been expressed and defended in many different ways. The first preaching and the first defense of the faith consisted in maintaining that Jesus of Nazareth is in truth the Messiah of Israel, and that the Messiah Himself — the Christ — is indeed truly Lord and God in human form. The first Christians, beginning with the apostles, had to insist on the fact that not only is Jesus truly the Christ and the Son of God, but that He has truly lived and died and risen from the dead in the flesh, as a true human being.

By this you know the Spirit of God: every spirit which confesses that Jesus Christ has come in the flesh is of God, and every spirit which does not confess Jesus is not of God. (1 John 4:2)

For many deceivers have gone into the world, men who will not acknowledge the coming of Jesus Christ in the flesh . . . (2 John 7)

In the early years of the Christian faith, the defenders of the faith — the apologists and martyrs — had as their central witness and task the defense of the doctrine that Jesus, being the Son of God in human flesh, has lived on earth, has died, has been raised by the Father and has been glorified as the only King and Lord and God of the world.

The Ecumenical Councils

In the third and fourth centuries attempts were made to teach that although Jesus is truly the incarnate Son and Word of God, that the Son and Word Himself is not fully and totally divine, but a creature — even the most exalted creature — but a creature made by God like everything else that was made. This was the teaching of the Arians. Against this teaching, the fathers, such as Athanasius of Alexandria, Basil the Great, his brother, Gregory of Nyssa, and Gregory the Theologian of Nazianzus defended the definition of faith of the first and second ecumenical councils which held that the Son and Word of God — incarnate in human form as Jesus of Nazareth, the Messiah-Christ of Israel — is not a creature, but is truly divine with the same divinity as God the Father and the Holy Spirit. This was the defense of the doctrine of the Holy Trinity (see Chapter III) which preserved for the Church of all ages the faith that Jesus is indeed the divine Son of God, of one essence with the Father and the Holy Spirit, one of the Holy Trinity.

At the same time, in the fourth century, it was also necessary for the Church to reject the teaching of a certain Appolinarius, who claimed that although Jesus was indeed the incarnate Son and Word of God, the incarnation consisted in the Word merely taking a human body and not the fullness of human nature. This was the doctrine that Jesus had no real human soul, no human mind, no human spirit, but that the divine Son of God, who exists eternally with the Father and the Spirit, merely dwelt in a human body, in human flesh, as in a temple. It is for this reason that every official doctrinal statement in the Ortho- dox Church, including all of the statements of the ecumenical councils, always insists that the Son of God became man of the Virgin Mary with a rational soul and body; in other words, that the Son of God really became human in the full meaning of the word and that Jesus Christ was and is a real human being, having and being everything that every human being has and is. This is nothing other than the teaching of the Gospels and the New Testament scriptures gen- erally.

> Since therefore the children share in flesh and blood, He Himself likewise partook of the same nature . . . (being) made like His brethren in every respect . . . (Hebrews 2:14-17)

The Nestorian Controversy

In the fifth century a long and difficult controversy developed over the true understanding of the person and nature of Jesus Christ. The third ecumenical council in Ephesus in 431, following the teaching of St. Cyril of Alexandria, was most concerned to defend the fact that the One who was born of the Virgin Mary was no one other than the divine Son of God in human flesh. It was necessary to defend this fact most explicitly because some in the Church, following Nestorius, the bishop of Constantinople, were teaching that the Virgin Mary should not be called **Theotokos** — a term already used in the Church's theology — because it was claimed that the Virgin gave birth to the man Jesus whom the Son of God had become in the incarnation, and not to the Son Himself. In this view it was held that there is a division between the Son of God born in eternity from God the Father and the Son of Man born from the Virgin in Bethlehem; and that although there is certainly a real "connection" between them, Mary merely gave birth to the man. As such, it was held, Mary could be called **Theotokos** only by some sort of symbolic and overly-pious stretching of the word, but that it is rather dogmatically accurate to call her **Christotokos** (the one who gave birth to the **Messiah**) or **Anthropotokos** (the one who gave birth to the Man that the Son of God has become in the incarnation).

St. Cyril of Alexandria and the fathers of the council in Ephesus rejected the Nestorian doctrine and claimed that the term **Theotokos** for the Virgin Mary is completely and totally accurate and must be retained if the Christian faith is to be properly confessed and the Christian life properly lived. The term must be defended because there can be no division of any sort between the eternal Son and Word of God, begotten of the Father before all ages, and Jesus Christ, the Son of Mary. Mary's child is the eternal and divine Son of God. He — and no one else — was born of her as a child. He — and no one else — was incarnate in human flesh from her. He — and no one else — became man in the manger in Bethlehem. There can be no "connection" or "conjunction" between God's Son and Mary's Son because they are in fact one and the same person. God's Son was born of Mary. God's Son is divine; He is God. Therefore, Mary gave birth to God in the flesh, to God as a man. Therefore, Mary is truly **Theotokos**. The battle cry of St. Cyril and the

Council in Ephesus was just this: The Son of God and the Son of Man — one Son!

The Council of Chalcedon

This teaching about Jesus Christ, the incarnate Son of God, was further elaborated and explained by the definition of the fourth ecumenical council in Chalcedon in 451. This was necessary because there was a tendency to stress the divine nature of Christ to such an extent that His true human nature was underplayed to the point almost of being rejected. At the fourth council the well-known formulation was made which says that Jesus Christ, the incarnate Son and Word of God is one person (or hypostasis) having two full and complete natures: human and divine. Inspired particularly by the letter of Saint Leo, the Pope of Rome, the fourth council insisted that Jesus is exactly what God the Father is in relation to His divinity. This was a direct reference to the Nicene Creed which claims that the Son of God is "of one essence with the Father," which simply means that what God the Father is, the Son is also: Light from Light, True God from True God. And the council insisted as well that in the incarnation the Son of God became exactly what all human beings are, confessing that Jesus Christ is also "of one essence" with all human being in respect to His humanity. This doctrine was and is defended as teaching nothing other than the apostolic faith as recorded in the Gospels and the New Testament writings, for example, those of the Apostle Paul:

> . . . though He was in the form of God, (Jesus) did not count equality with God a thing to be clung to, but emptied Himself, taking on the form of a servant, being found in the likeness of men. And being found in human form He humbled Himself and became obedient unto death, even death on a cross. (Philippians 2:6-8; See also Hebrews 1-2, John 1)

The critical words in the definition of faith of the

Council of Chalcedon are the following:

Following the holy fathers we teach with one voice that the Son of God and our Lord Jesus Christ is to be confessed as one and the same (Person), and He is perfect in Divinity and perfect in Humanity, true God and true Man, of a rational soul and (human) body consisting, of one essence with the Father as touching His Divinity and of one essence with us as touching His Humanity; made in all things like unto us, with the exception of sin only; begotten of His Father before all ages according to His Divinity: but in these last days, for us men and for our salvation, born (into the world) of the Virgin Mary, Theotokos, according to His Humanity. This one and the same Jesus Christ, the only-begotten Son (of God) must be confessed to be in two natures, without mixture and without change, without separation and without division (i.e., without fusing together Divinity and Humanity so that the proper characteristics of each are changed or lost; and also without separating them in such a way that there might be considered to be two Sons and not One Son only) and that without the distinction of natures being removed by such union, but rather that the peculiar property of each nature being preserved and being united in one Person and Hypostasis, not separated or divided into two persons, but one and the same Son and only begotten, God the Word, our Lord Jesus Christ, as the Prophets of old have spoken concerning Him (e.g., the Immanuel of Isaiah 7:14), and as Jesus Christ has taught us, and as the Creed of the fathers has delivered to us.

A number of Christians did not accept the Council of Chalcedon and broke communion with those who did accept it. They did so because they thought that the council had in fact resurrected the wrong doctrine of Nestorius by insisting on the "two natures" after the incarnation, however strongly and firmly the "union" of the two natures was insisted upon. These Christians were called the **monophysites** (from the term meaning "one nature" after the incarnation), and they continue until today in separation from the Chalcedonian Orthodox in the Coptic, Ethiopian and Armenian churches. Hopefully, one day, by God's grace, this dispute will be resolved and those who adhere to Chalcedon — the Eastern Orthodox Christians, as well as the traditional Roman Catholics and Protestants — will come to a unity of faith with those who reject Chalcedon in regard to its explication of the union of the divine and the human in the one person of Christ our Lord. Whatever the future may hold by God's grace, however, it is still the firm teaching of the Orthodox Church that the Council of Chalcedon is in strict adherence with the anti-Nestorian doctrines of Saint Cyril and the third ecumenical council in Ephesus. The virtue of the fourth council, in the Orthodox view, is that it defines very clearly the fact that when the Son of God was born as a man from the Virgin Mary, Theotokos, He did not cease to be God or change in His Divinity, while becoming a complete and perfect man in His incarnate Humanity. For salvation itself requires the perfect union of Divinity and Humanity in the one Person of Jesus Christ; a union where God is God and Man is Man, and yet where the two become one in perfect unity: without fusion or change, and without division or separation.

Emperor Justinian and the 5th Ecumenical Council

In the sixth century, the Byzantine Emperor Justinian wanted to reaffirm the fact that the followers of the council of Chalcedon really believed that Jesus Christ is the incarnate Son and Word of God, one of the Holy Trinity. He wanted to do this primarily to convince those who did not accept the fourth council that its definition did not reintroduce the error of Nestorius. To do this, the Emperor called the council now known as the fifth ecumenical council in Constantinople in 553 which further served to clarify the Orthodox position in regard to the person and action of Christ. The following are some of the key texts of this council:

If anyone understands the expression "one Person only of our Lord Jesus Christ" in this sense, that it is the union of many hypostases (or persons), and if he thus attempts to introduce into the mystery of Christ two hypostases or two persons, and after having introduced two persons speaks of one Person only in the sense of dignity, honor or worship . . . (and) shall calumniate the holy council of Chalcedon, pretending that it used this expression (one hypostasis and person) in this impious sense . . . let him be anathema.

If anyone shall not call in a true acceptation . . . the holy, glorious and ever-virgin Mary, the Theotokos . . . believing that she bare only a simple man and that God the Word was not incarnate of her . . . (and) shall calumniate the holy synod of Chalcedon as though it has asserted the Virgin to be Theotokos according to the impious sense . . . let him be anathema.

If anyone using the expression "in two natures" does not confess that our one Lord Jesus Christ has been revealed in the divinity and in the humanity, so as to designate by that expression a difference of the natures of which an ineffable union is made without confusion, in which neither the nature of the Word was changed into that of the flesh, nor that of the flesh into that of the Word, for each remained what it was by nature, the union being hypostatic (i.e., in the one Person); but shall take the expression to divide the parties . . . let him be anathema.

If anyone does not confess that our Lord Jesus Christ who was crucified in the flesh is true God and the Lord of Glory and one of the Holy Trinity, let him be anathema.

To further emphasize the point that the Chalcedonian Council was truly orthodox, the Emperor Justinian wrote a doctrinal hymn which is still sung in the Orthodox Church at every divine liturgy. It confesses the Lord Jesus Christ as perfect God and perfect man.

Only-begotten Son and Word of God,
Who for our salvation willed to be incarnate of the holy Theotokos and ever-virgin Mary,
Who without change became man and was crucified,
Who is one of the Holy Trinity, glorified with the Father and the Holy Spirit,
O Christ our God, trampling down death by death,
Save us!

The Monothelite Controversy

In the seventh century the question of how to understand, define and confess the person and action of Jesus Christ continued to cause divisions among the believers. Some now said that after the Son of God became man, He had just one activity and will – the theandric activity and will of the Word-made-flesh. These people, called **monothelites,** insisted that the One Person of Christ, in uniting the natures of God and Man in His One Person, fused together the human and divine will and activity in such a way that they no longer could be distinguished.

The sixth ecumenical council met in Constantinople in 680-681. Following the teachings of St. Maximus the Confessor who was imprisoned and tortured for his doctrines, it decreed that just as Christ is really fully divine and fully human, the perfect union of Divinity and Humanity in one Person, so also He must have both a real human activity and will and a real divine activity and will — according to each of His natures — and that these two wills and activities, like the natures themselves, should not be understood to be fused or mingled together into one so as to lose their proper natural characteristics and properties. This decision was based on the fact that since the Son of God remained fully divine in the incarnation, He must continue to have His proper divine activity and will; and that since He became fully human in the incarnation He must also have a complete and perfect human activity and will; and that the salvation of mankind requires that the distinction — but not the division or separation — of each of these respective activities and wills remain in the incarnate Saviour. The following is part of the definition of faith of the sixth council:

> . . . in Him are two natural wills and two natural operations without division, without fusion, without change and without separation according to the teaching of the holy fathers. And these two natural wills are not contrary to one another (God forbid!) . . . but His human will follows, and not as resisting and reluctant, but rather as subject to His divine and omnipotent will . . . [. . .] For as His most holy and immaculate animated flesh was not destroyed because it was deified but continued in its own state and nature, so also His human will, although deified, was not suppressed, but was rather preserved . . . We glorify two natural operations . . . in the same Lord Jesus Christ our true God, that is to say a divine operation [or action] and a human operation [or action] . . . For we will not admit one natural operation in God and in the creature. [. . .] . . . believing our Lord Jesus Christ to be one of the Trinity, and after the incarnation our true God we say that His two natures shone forth in His one hypostasis [or person] in which

He both performed the miracles and endured the sufferings . . . [. . .] Wherefore we confess two wills and two operations concurring most fitly in Him for the salvation of the human race.

Iconoclastic Controversy

In the eighth and ninth centuries the question of the person and nature of Christ continued in the controversy over the veneration of the holy icons in the Church. At this time many were found, including emperors and secular rulers, who claimed that the veneration of icons is wrong because it is the sin of idolatry. They claimed that as God is invisible and has commanded in the Old Testament law that men are not to make "graven images," so it is wrong to depict and to honor images of Christ and the saints.

The defenders of the veneration of the holy icons, led by Saints John Damascene and Theodore Studion, claimed that the central point of the Christian faith is that **"the Word became flesh and dwelt among us"** and that **"we have beheld His glory." (John 1:14)** Referring to the holy scriptures they insisted that belief in the incarnation of the Son of God calls for the veneration of icons since Jesus Christ is a real man with a real human soul and body, and as such can be depicted. They said that those who were against the holy icons reduced the incarnation to a "fantasy" and denied the true humanity of the Son of God in His coming to man. Thus they made reference to the words of Jesus Himself in His dialogue with Philip:

Philip said to Him, "Lord, show us the Father and we shall be satisfied."

Jesus said to him, "Have I been with you so long, and yet you do not know me, Philip? He who has seen me has seen the Father; how can you say, 'Show us the Father?'" (John 14:8-9)

The defenders of the propriety of icon veneration also referred to the apostolic writings of Saint John and Saint Paul:

83

That which was from the beginning, which we
have heard, which we have seen with our eyes,
which we have looked upon and touched with
our hands concerning the Word of Life — the
Life was made manifest, and we saw it . . .
(1 John 1:1-2)

. . . the god of this world has blinded the minds
of the unbelievers to keep them from seeing the
light of the gospel of the glory of Christ, who is
the likeness [in Greek: eikon] of God. (2 Corinthians 4:4)

He is the image [in Greek: eikon] of the invisible
God, the first born of all creation; for in Him all
things were created, in heaven and on earth . . .
all things were created through Him and for Him
. . . for in Him all the fullness of God was pleased
to dwell . . . (Colossians 1:15-20)

In many and various ways God spoke of old to
our fathers by the prophets, but in these last
days He has spoken to us by a Son, whom He
appointed the heir of all things, through whom
also He created the world. He is the reflection of
the glory of God and the express image of His
person, upholding the universe by the word of
His power . . . (Hebrews 1:1-3)

The seventh ecumenical council in Nicea in 787 officially declared that the Christian faith is to be proclaimed "in words and images." And while making
clear the teaching that holy icons may be made; that
they are not to be worshipped — for only God Himself is worthy of worship — but are to be venerated
and honored; the seventh council also made the following statement about Christ in reference to the
veneration of icons:

. . . we keep unchanged all the ecclesiastical traditions handed down to us, whether in writing or
verbally, one of which is the making of pictorial
representations, agreeable to the history of the

preaching of the Gospel, a tradition useful in many respects, but especially in this, that so the incarnation of the Word of God is shone forth in real and not merely in phantasy, for these have mutual indications and without doubt have also mutual significations.

In later times the doctrines of the real divinity and real humanity of Jesus Christ was witnessed and defended by such saints as Simeon the New Theologian (d. 1022) and Gregory Palamas, the Archbishop of Thessalonika (d. 1359) in their teachings about the real sanctification and deification of man through living communion with God through Jesus Christ in the Holy Spirit in the Church. In and through Christ, the Word incarnate, human persons can be filled with the Spirit of God and can be in genuine communion with God the Father, participating in the uncreated being, life and light of the Most Blessed Trinity. If Jesus Christ were not true God and true Man, this would be impossible. But it is not impossible. It is man's experience of salvation and redemption in the life of the Church of Christ.

Redemption

And He was crucified for us under Pontius Pilate, and suffered, and was buried

Although Jesus did not sin and did not have to suffer and die, he voluntarily took upon himself the sins of the world and voluntarily gave himself up to suffering and death for the sake of salvation. This was his task as the Messiah-Saviour:

> The Spirit of the Lord is upon me to bring good tidings to the afflicted...to bind up the broken-hearted, to proclaim liberty to the captives, and the opening of the prison to those who are bound...to comfort all who mourn...to give them a garland instead of ashes, the oil of gladness instead of mourning." (Isaiah 61:1-3)

And at the same time, Jesus had to do this as the suffering servant of Yahweh-God.

> He was despised and rejected by men, a man of sorrows, and acquainted with grief, and as one from whom men hide their faces he was despised. and we esteemed him not.

> Surely he has borne our griefs and carried our sorrows, yet we esteemed him stricken, smitten by God and afflicted.

> But he was wounded for our transgressions, he was bruised for our iniquities, upon him was the chastisement that made us whole, and by his stripes (i.e. wounds) we are healed.

> All we like sheep have gone astray; we have turned everyone to his own way; and the Lord has laid on him the iniquity of us all.

> He was oppressed, and he was afflicted, yet he opened not his mouth; like a lamb led to the slaughter, and like a sheep that before his shearers is dumb, so he opened not his mouth.

> By oppression and judgement he was taken away ...And they made his grave with the wicked, and with a rich man in his death, although he had done no violence, and there was no deceit in his mouth.

> Yet it was the will of the Lord (Yahweh) to
> bruise him; he has put him to grief; when he
> makes himself an offering for sin, he shall see
> his offspring, he shall prolong his days; the will
> of the Lord shall propser in his hand; he shall see
> the fruit of the travail of his soul and be satisfied;
> by his knowledge shall the righteous one, my
> servant, make many to be accounted righteous;
> and he shall bear their iniquities.
>
> Therefore I will divide him a portion with the
> great and he shall divide the spoil with the
> strong; because he poured out his soul to death,
> and was numbered with the transgressors; yet he
> bore the sin of many (or the multitude) and made
> intercession for the transgressors. (Isaiah 53)

These words of the prophet Isaiah written centuries
before the birth of Jesus tell the story of his Messianic
mission. It began officially before the eyes of all in his
baptism by John in the Jordan. By allowing himself to
be baptized with the sinners though he had no sin,
Jesus shows that he accepts his calling to be identified
with the sinners: "the Beloved" of the Father and
"the Lamb of God who takes away the sin of the
world." (John 1:29; Matthew 3:17)

Jesus begins to teach, and on the very day and at that
very moment when his disciples first confess him to
be the Messiah, "the Christ, the Son of the Living
God," Jesus tells immediately of his mission to "go to
Jerusalem and suffer many things...and be killed, and
on the third day be raised." (Matthew 16:16-23; Mark
8:29-33) The apostles are greatly upset by this. Jesus
then immediately shows them his divinity by being
transfigured before them in divine glory on the moun-
tain in the presence of Moses and Elijah. He then tells
them once more: "The Son of Man is to be delivered
into the hands of men, and they will kill him, and he
will be raised on the third day." (Matthew 17:1-23;
Mark 9:1-9)

The powers of evil multiplied against Christ at the end: "**The kings of the earth counsel together against the Lord and His Christ.**" (Psalm 2:2) They were looking for causes to kill him. The formal reason was blasphemy, "**because you, being a man, make yourself God.**" (John 10:31-38) Yet the deep reasons were more personal: Jesus told men the truth and revealed their stubbornness, foolishness, hypocrisy and sin. For this reason every sinner, hardened in his sins and refusing to repent, wishes and causes the crucifixion of Christ.

The death of Jesus came at the hands of the religious and political leaders of his time, with the approval of the masses: when Caiaphas was high priest, "under Pontius Pilate." He was "crucified for us...and suffered and was buried" in order to be with us in our sufferings and death which we brought upon ourselves because of our sins: "**for the wages of sin are death.**" (**Romans 6:23**) In this sense the Apostle Paul writes of Jesus that "**having become a curse for us**" (**Galations 3:13**), "**for our sake he** (God the Father) **made him to be sin who knew no sin, so that in him we might become the righteousness of God.**" (**II Corinthians 5:21**)

The sufferings and death of Christ in obedience to the Father reveals the super-abundant divine love of God for his creation. For when all was sinful, cursed and dead, Christ became sin, a curse and dead for us—though he himself never ceased to be the righteousness and blessedness and life of God Himself. It is to this depth, of which lower and more base cannot be discovered or imagined, that Christ has humiliated himself "for us men and for our salvation." For being God, he became man; and being man, he became a slave; and being a slave, he became dead and not only dead, but dead on a cross. From this deepest degradation of God flows the eternal exaltation of man. This is the pivotal doctrine of the Orthodox Christian faith,

expressed over and again in many ways throughout the history of the Orthodox Church. It is the doctrine of the **atonement** — for we are made to be "at one" with God. It is the doctrine of **redemption** — for we are redeemed, i.e., **"bought with a price,"** the great price of the blood of God. (Acts 20:28; I Corinthians 6:20)

> **Have this mind among yourselves which you have in Christ Jesus who, though He was in the form of God, did not count equality with God a thing to be grasped, but emptied Himself, taking the form of a servant (slave), being born in the likeness of men. And being found in human form, He humbled Himself and became obedient unto death, even death on a cross. Therefore God has highly exalted Him and bestowed on Him the name which is above every name, that at the name of Jesus every knee should bow, in heaven and on earth and under the earth, and every tongue confess that Jesus Christ is Lord, to the glory of God the Father. (Philippians 2:5-11)**

In contemplating the saving and redeeming action of Christ, it has become traditional to emphasize three aspects which in reality are not divided, and cannot be; but which in theory (i.e., in the **vision** of Christ's being and activity as the Saviour of the world) may be distinguished. The first of these three aspects of the redeeming work of Christ is the fact that Jesus saves mankind by providing the perfect image and example of human life as filled with the grace and power of God.

Jesus, the Perfect Image of Human Life

Christ is the incarnate Word of God. He is the Teacher and Master sent by God to the world. He is the embodiment of God Himself in human form. He is **"the image of the invisible God."** (Colossians 1:15) In Him **"the fullness of divinity dwells bodily."** (Colossians 2:9) The person who sees Jesus sees God the Father.

(John 14:9) He is the "**reflection of the glory of God and the express image of His person.**" (Hebrews 1:3) He is the "**light of the world**" who "**enlightens every man . . . coming into the world.**" (John 8:12, 1:9) To be saved by Jesus Christ is first of all to be enlightened by Him; to see Him as the Light, and to see all things in the light of Him. It is to know Him as "**the Truth**" (**John 14:6**); and to know the truth in Him.

> **And you will know the truth and the truth will make you free. (John 8:31)**

When one is saved by God in Christ one comes to the knowledge of the truth, fulfilling God's desire for His creatures, for "**God our Saviour . . . desires all men to be saved and to come to the knowledge of the truth.**" (**1 Timothy 2:4**) In saving God's world, Jesus Christ enlightens God's creatures by the Holy Spirit, the Spirit of God who is the Spirit of Truth who proceeds from the Father and is sent into the world through Christ.

> **If you love Me, you will keep My commandments. And I will pray the Father, and He will give you another Counselor, to be with you forever, even the Spirit of Truth, whom the world cannot receive, because it neither sees Him nor knows Him; you know Him, for He dwells with you, and will be in you. (John 14:15-17)**

> **But the Counselor, the Holy Spirit, whom the Father will send in My name, He will teach you all things, and bring to your remembrance all that I have said to you . . . (John 15:26)**

> **When the Spirit of Truth comes, He will guide you into all the truth . . . (John 16:13)**

The first aspect of salvation in Christ, therefore, is to be enlightened by Him and to know the truth about God and man by the guidance of the Holy Spirit, the Spirit of Truth, which God gives through Him to those who believe. This is witnessed to in the apostolic writings of Saints John and Paul:

Now we have received not the spirit of the world, but the Spirit which is from God, that we might understand the gifts bestowed on us by God. And we impart this in words not taught by human wisdom, but taught by the Spirit, interpreting spiritual truths to those who possess the Spirit. [. . .] For who has known the mind of the Lord so as to instruct him? But we have the mind of Christ. (1 Corinthians 2:13-16)

For (God) has made known to us in all wisdom and insight the mystery of His will, according to His purpose which He set forth in Christ as a plan for the fullness of time, to unite all things in Him, things in heaven and things on earth. [. . .] To me . . . this grace was given . . . to make all men see what is the plan of the mystery hidden for ages in God . . . that through the church the manifold wisdom of God might now be made known . . . (Ephesians 1:8-10; 3:9)

For I want . . . that their hearts may be encouraged as they are knit together in love, to have all the riches of assured understanding and the knowledge of God's mystery in Christ, in whom are hid all the treasures of wisdom and knowledge. (Colossians 2:1-3)

But you have been anointed by the Holy One, and you know all things. I write to you, not because you do not know the truth, but because you know it, and know that no lie is of the truth. [. . .] . . . but the anointing which you received from Him abides in you, and you have no need that any one should teach you; as His anointing teaches you about everything, and is true and is no lie, just as it has taught you, abide in Him. [. . .] And by this we know that He abides in us, by the Spirit which He has given to us. (1 John 2:20-27; 3:24)

The first aspect of man's salvation by God in Christ is, therefore, the ability and power to see, to know, to believe and to love the truth of God in Christ, who is the Truth, by the Spirit of Truth. It is the gift of knowledge and wisdom, of illumination and enlightenment. It is the condition of being "taught by God" as foretold by the prophets and fulfilled by Christ. (Isaiah 54:13; Jeremiah 31:33-34; John 6:45) Thus, in the Orthodox Church, the entrance into the saving life of the Church through baptism and chrismation is called "holy illumination." (See Book II on *Worship*)

For it is God who said, "Let light shine out of darkness," who has shone in our hearts to give the light of the knowledge of the glory of God in the face of Christ. (2 Corinthians 4:6)

Jesus, the Reconciler of Man with God

The second aspect of Christ's one, indivisible act of salvation of man and his world is the accomplishment of man's reconciliation with God the Father through the forgiveness of sins. This is the **redemption** and **atonement** strictly speaking, the release from sins, and the punishment due to sins; the being made "at one" with God.

While we were yet helpless, at the right time Christ died for the ungodly. Why, one will hardly die for a righteous man — though perhaps for a good man one will dare even to die. But God shows His love for us in that while we were yet sinners Christ died for us. Since therefore we are now made righteous by His blood, much more shall we be saved by Him from the wrath of God. For if while we were enemies we were reconciled to God by the death of His Son, much more, now that we are reconciled, shall we be saved by His life. Not only so, but we also rejoice in God through our Lord Jesus Christ, through whom we have now received our reconciliation. (Romans 5:6-11)

> Therefore if anyone is in Christ, he is a new crea-
> tion; the old has passed away, behold, the new
> has come. All this is from God, who through
> Christ reconciled us to Himself and gave us the
> ministry of reconciliation; that is, God was in
> Christ reconciling the world to Himself, not
> counting their trespasses against them, and en-
> trusting to us the message of reconciliation.
> (2 Corinthians 5:17-19)

The forgiveness of sins is one of the signs of the coming of the Christ, the Messiah, as foretold in the Old
Testament.

> . . . they shall all know me, from the least to the
> greatest, says the Lord; for I will forgive their
> iniquity, and I will remember their sin no more.
> (Jeremiah 31:34)

Christ is the Lamb of God who takes away the sins of
the world, the Lamb that is slain that through Him all
sins might be forgiven. He is also the great high priest,
who offers the perfect sacrifice by which man is
purged from his sins and cleansed from his iniquities.
Jesus offers, as high priest, the perfect sacrifice of His
own very life, His own body, as the Lamb of God,
upon the tree of the cross.

> For to this you have been called, because Christ
> suffered for you, leaving you an example that
> you should follow in His steps. He committed no
> sin; no guile was found on His lips. When He was
> reviled, He did not revile in return; when He
> suffered, He did not threaten; but He trusted to
> Him who judges justly. He Himself bore our sins
> in His body on the tree, that we might die to sin
> and live to righteousness. By His wounds you
> have been healed. For you were straying like
> sheep, but have now returned to the Pastor and
> Bishop of your souls. (1 Peter 2:22-25)

The high-priestly offering and sacrifice of the Son of God to His eternal Father is described in great detail in the Letter to the Hebrews in the New Testament scriptures.

> In the days of His flesh, Jesus offered up prayers and supplications, with loud cries and tears, to Him who was able to save Him from death, and He was heard for His godly fear. Although He was a Son, He learned obedience through what He suffered, and being made perfect, He became the source of eternal salvation to all who obey Him, being designated a high priest by God, according to the order of Melchizedek. (Hebrews 5:7-10)

> But when Christ appeared as a high priest of the good things that have come . . . He entered once for all into the Holy Place (not made by hands, i.e., the Presence of God) taking . . . His own blood, thus securing an eternal redemption. For if the sprinkling of defiled persons with the blood of goats and bulls and with the ashes of a heifer sanctifies for the purification of the flesh, how much more shall the blood of Christ who through the eternal Spirit offered Himself without blemish to God, purify your conscience from dead works to serve the living God. Therefore, He is the mediator of a new covenant, so that those who are called may receive the promised eternal inheritance, since a death has occurred which redeems them from the transgressions under the first covenant. (Hebrews 9:11-15)

According to the scriptures, man's sins and the sins of the whole world are forgiven and pardoned by the sacrifice of Christ, by the offering of His life — His body and His blood, which is the "blood of God" (Acts 20:28) — upon the cross. This is the "redemption," the "ransom," the "expiation," the "propitiation" spoken about in the scriptures which had to be made so that man could be **"at one"** with God. Christ **"paid the price"** which was necessary to be paid for the world to be pardoned and cleansed of all iniquities and sins. (1 Corinthians 6:20; 7:23)

In the history of Christian doctrine there has been great debate over the question of to whom Christ "pays the price" for the ransom of the world and the salvation of mankind. Some have said that the "payment" was made to the devil. This is the view that the devil received certain "rights" over man and his world because of man's sin. In his rebellion against God, man "sold himself to the devil" thus allowing the Evil One to become the **"prince of this world." (John 12:31)** Christ comes to pay the debt to the devil and to release man from his control by sacrificing Himself upon the cross.

Others say that Christ's "payment" on behalf of man had to be made to God the Father. This is the view which interprets Christ's sacrificial death on the cross as the proper punishment that had to be paid to satisfy God's wrath over the human race. God was insulted by man's sin. His law was broken and His righteousness was offended. Man had to pay the penalty for his sin by offering the proper punishment. But no amount of human punishment could satisfy God's justice because God's justice is divine. Thus the Son of God had to be born into the world and receive the punishment that was rightly to be placed on men. He had to die in order for God to receive proper satisfaction for man's offenses against Him. Christ substituted Himself on our behalf and died for our sins, offering His blood as the satisfying sacrifice for the sins of the world. By dying on the cross in place of sinful man, Christ pays the full and total payment for man's sins. God's wrath is removed. Man's insult is punished. The world is reconciled with its Creator.

Commenting on this question about to whom Christ "pays the price" for man's salvation, St. Gregory the

Theologian in the fourth century wrote the following in his second Easter Oration:

Now we are to examine another fact and dogma, neglected by most people, but in my judgment well worth enquiring into. To whom was that Blood offered that was shed for us, and why was It shed? I mean the precious and famous Blood of our God and High Priest and Sacrifice.

We were detained in bondage by the Evil One, sold under sin, and receiving pleasure in exchange for wickedness. Now, since a ransom belongs only to him who holds in bondage, I ask to whom was this offered, and for what cause?

If to the Evil One, fie upon the outrage! If the robber receives ransom, not only from God, but a ransom which consists of God Himself, and has such an illustrious payment for his tyranny, then it would have been right for him to have left us alone altogether!

But if to God the Father, I ask first, how? For it was not by Him that we were being oppressed. And next, on what principle did the Blood of His only-begotten Son delight the Father, who would not receive even Isaac, when he was being sacrificed by his father, (Abraham), but changed the sacrifice by putting a ram in the place of the human victim? (See Genesis 22)

Is it not evident that the Father accepts Him, but neither asked for Him nor demanded Him; but on account of the incarnation, and because Humanity must be sanctified by the Humanity of God, that He might deliver us Himself, and overcome the tyrant (i.e., the devil) and draw us to Himself by the mediation of His Son who also arranged this to the honor of the Father, whom it is manifest He obeys in all things.

In Orthodox theology generally it can be said that the language of "payment" and "ransom" is rather understood as a metaphorical and symbolical way of saying that Christ has done all things necessary to save and redeem mankind enslaved to the devil, sin and death, and under the wrath of God. He "paid the price," not in some legalistic or juridical or economic meaning. He "paid the price" not to the devil whose rights over man were won by deceit and tyranny. He "paid the price" not to God the Father in the sense that God delights in His sufferings and received "satisfaction" from His creatures in Him. He "paid the price" rather, we might say, to Reality Itself. He "paid the price" to create the conditions in and through which man might receive the forgiveness of sins and eternal life by dying and rising again in Him to newness of life. (See Romans 5-8; Galatians 2-4)

By dying on the cross and rising from the dead, Jesus Christ cleansed the world from evil and sin. He defeated the devil "in his own territory" and on "his own terms." The **wages of sin is death." (Romans 6:23)** So the Son of God became man and took upon Himself the sins of the world and died a voluntary death. By His sinless and innocent death accomplished entirely by His free will — and not by physical, moral, or juridical necessity — He made death to die and to become itself the source and the way into life eternal. This is what the Church sings on the feast of the Resurrection, the New Passover in Christ, the new Paschal Lamb, who is risen from the dead:

> **Christ is risen from the dead!**
> **Trampling down death by death!**
> **And upon those in the tombs bestowing life!**
>   **(Easter Troparion)**

And this is how the Church prays at the divine liturgy of Saint Basil the Great:

> **He was God before the ages, yet He appeared on earth and lived among men, becoming incarnate of a holy Virgin;**

He emptied Himself, taking the form of a servant, being likened to the body of our lowliness,
that He might liken us to the image of His Glory.

For as by man sin entered into the world, and
death by sin, so it pleased Thine Only-begotten
Son, who was in the bosom of Thee, the God
and Father, who was born of a woman, the holy
Theotokos and ever-virgin Mary, who was born
under the law to condemn sin in His flesh, so
that those who were dead in Adam might be
made alive in Thy Christ Himself.

He lived in this world and gave commandments
of salvation; releasing us from the delusions of
idolatry, He brought us to knowledge of Thee,
the true God and Father. He obtained us for His
own chosen people, a royal priesthood, a holy
nation.

Having cleansed us in water, and sanctified us
with the Holy Spirit, He gave Himself as a ransom to death, in which we were held captive,
sold under sin.

Descending through the cross into Sheol — that
He might fill all things with Himself — He loosed
the pangs of death. He arose on the third day,
having made for all flesh a path to the resurrection from the dead, since it was not possible for
the Author of Life to be a victim of corruption.

So He became the first-fruits of those who have
fallen asleep, the first-born of the dead, that He
might be Himself truly the first in all things . . .
(Eucharistic Prayer of the Liturgy of St. Basil)

Jesus, the Destroyer of Death

The third and final aspect of the saving and redeeming
action of Christ, therefore, is the deepest and most
comprehensive. It is the destruction of death by
Christ's own death. It is the transformation of death
itself into an act of life. It is the recreation of Sheol —

the spiritual condition of being dead — into the paradise of God. Thus, in and through the death of Jesus Christ, death is made to die. In Him, who is the Resurrection and the Life, man cannot die, but lives forever with God.

Truly, truly I say to you, he who hears my word and believes in Him who sent me has eternal life; he does not come into judgment, but has passed from death into life. (John 5:24)

"I am the Resurrection and the Life! He who believes in me, though he die, yet shall he live, and whoever lives and believes in me shall never die." (John 11:25-26)

It is Christ Jesus who died, yes, who was raised from the dead, who is at the right hand of God, who indeed intercedes for us! Who shall separate us from the love of Christ? [. . .] For I am sure that neither death, nor life, nor angels, nor principalities, nor things present, nor things to come, nor powers, nor height, nor depth, nor anything else in all creation will be able to separate us from the love of God in Christ Jesus our Lord. (Romans 8:34-39)

For in Him the whole fullness of divinity dwells bodily, and you have come to fullness of life in Him . . . and you were buried with Him in baptism, in which you were also raised with Him through faith in the working of God who raised Him from the dead. And you were dead in trespasses . . . God made alive together with Him, having forgiven us all our trespasses, having cancelled the bond which stood against us with its legal demands; this He set aside, nailing it to the cross. He disarmed the (demonic) principalities and powers and made a public example of them, triumphing over them . . . for you have died, and your life is hid with Christ in God. (Colossians 2:9 ff.)

This is the doctrine of the New Testament scriptures, repeated over and again in many ways in the tradition of the Church: in its sacraments, hymnology, theology, iconography. Christ's victory over death is man's release from sins and man's victory over enslavement to the devil because in and through Christ's death man dies and is born again to eternal life. In his death sins are no longer counted. In his death the devil no longer holds him. In his death he is born again to newness of life and is liberated from all that is evil, false, demonic and sinful. In a word, he is freed from all that is dead by dying and rising again in and with Jesus.

But we see Jesus, who for a little while was made lower than the angels, crowned with glory and honor because of the suffering of death, so that by the grace of God He might taste death for every one. [. . .] Since therefore the children share in flesh and blood, He Himself likewise partook of the same nature, that through death He might destroy him who has the power of death, that is, the devil, and deliver all those who through fear of death were subject to lifelong bondage. (Hebrews 2:9-15)

But in fact Christ has been raised from the dead, the first-fruits of those who have fallen asleep. For as by a man came death, by a Man has come also the resurrection of the dead. For as in Adam all die, so also in Christ shall all be made alive. [. . .] The sting of death is sin, and the power of sin is the law. But thanks be to God who gives us the victory through our Lord Jesus Christ. (1 Corinthians 15:20 ff; 56-57)

Resurrection

And He rose again from the dead on the third day, according to the Scriptures

Christ is risen from the dead! This is the main proclamation of the Christian faith. It forms the heart of the Church's preaching, worship and spiritual life. "...if Christ has not been raised, then our preaching is in vain and your faith is in vain." (I Corinthians 15:14)

In the first sermon ever preached in the history of the Christian Church, the Apostle Peter began his proclamation:

> Men of Israel, hear these words; Jesus of Nazareth, a man attended to you by God with mighty works and signs and wonders which God did to him in your midst, as you yourself know—this Jesus delivered up according to a definite plan and foreknowledge of God, you crucified and killed by the hands of lawless men. But God raised him up, having loosed the pains of death, because it was not possible for him to be held by it. (Acts 2:22-24)

Jesus had the power to lay down his life and the power to take it up again:

> For this reason the Father loves me, because I lay down my life, that I may take it again. No one takes it from me, but I lay it down of my own accord. I have the power to lay it down, and I have the power to take it again; this charge I have received from my father. (John 10:17-18)

According to Orthodox doctrine there is no competition of "lives" between God and Jesus, and no competition of "powers." The power of God and the power of Jesus, the life of God and the life of Jesus. are one and the same power and life. To say that God has raised Christ, and that Christ has been raised by his own power is to say essentially the same thing. "For as the Father has life in himself," says Christ, so he has granted the Son also to have life in himself." (John 5:26) "I and the Father are one." (John 10:30)

The Scriptural stress that God has raised up Jesus only emphasizes once more that Christ has given his life, that he has laid it down fully, that he has offered it whole and without reservation to God--who then gave it back in his resurrection from the dead.

The Orthodox Church believes in Christ's real death and his actual resurrection. Resurrection, however, does not simply mean bodily resusitation. Neither the Gospel nor the Church teaches that Jesus was lying dead and then was biologically revived and walked around in the same way that he did before he was killed. In a word, the Gospel does not say that the angel moved the stone from the tomb in order to let Jesus out. The angel moved the stone to reveal that Jesus was not there. (Mark 16; Matthew 28)

In his resurrection Jesus is in a new and glorious form. He appears in different places immediately. He is difficult to recognize. (Luke 24:16; John 20:14) He eats and drinks to show that he is not a ghost. (Luke 24:30, 39) He allows himself to be touched. (John 20:27, 21:9) And yet he appears in the midst of disciples, **"the doors being shut," (John 20:19, 26)** And he **"vanishes out of their sight." (Luke 24:31)** Christ indeed is risen, but his resurrected humanity is full of life and divinity. It is humanity in the new form of the eternal life of the Kingdom of God.

So it is with the resurrection of the dead. What is sown is perishable, what is raised is imperishable. It is sown in dishonor, it is raised in glory. It is sown in weakness, it is raised in power. It is sown a physical body, it is raised a spiritual body.

Thus, it is written, the first man Adam became a living being; the last Adam (i.e. Christ) became a life-giving spirit. But it is not the spiritual which is first but the physical, then the spiritual.

The first man was from the earth, a man of dust; the second man is from heaven. As was the man

On Death and Resurrection in Christ

Yesterday I was crucified with Him; today I am glorified with Him.

Yesterday I died with Him; today I am made alive with Him.

Yesterday I was buried with Him; today I am raised up with Him.

Let us offer to Him Who suffered and rose again for us . . . *ourselves*, the possession most precious to God and most proper.

Let us become like Christ, since Christ became like us.

Let us become Divine for His sake, since for us He became Man.

He assumed the worse that He might give us the better.
He became poor that by His poverty we might become rich.
He accepted the form of a servant that we might win back our freedom.
He came down that we might be lifted up.
He was tempted that through Him we might conquer.
He was dishonored that He might glorify us.
He died that He might save us.
He ascended that He might draw to Himself us, who were thrown down through the fall of sin.

Let us give all, offer all, to Him who gave Himself a Ransom and Reconciliation for us.

We needed an incarnate God, a God put to death, that we might live. We were put to death together with Him that we might be cleansed. We rose again with Him because we were put to death with Him. We were glorified with Him because we rose again with Him.

A few drops of Blood recreate the whole of creation!

St. Gregory the Theologian
Easter Orations

of dust, so are those who are of the dust; and as
is the man from heaven, so are those who are of
heaven. Just as we have borne the image of the
man of dust, we shall also bear the image of the
man of heaven. (I Corinthians 15:42-50)

The resurrection of Christ is the first fruits of the resurrection of all humanity. It is the fulfillment of the
Old Testament, "according to the Scriptures" where
it is written, "For Thou doest not give me up unto
Sheol (that is, the realm of death), or let Thy Godly
one see corruption." (Psalm 16:10; Acts 2:25-36) In
Christ all expectations and hopes are filled: O Death,
where is your sting? O Sheol, where is your victory?
(Hosea 13:34)

He will swallow up death forever, and the Lord
God will wipe away tears from all faces . . . It
will be said on that day, "Lo, this is our God; we
have waited for Him; let us be glad and rejoice in
His salvation." (Isaiah 25:8-9)

Come, let us return to the Lord:
For He has torn, that He may heal us;
He has stricken, and He will bind us up.
After two days He will revive us;
On the third day He will raise us up,
    that we may live before Him. (Hosea 6:1-2)

Thus says the Lord God: Behold I will open your
    graves, and raise you from your graves, O my
    people . . .
And you shall know that I am the Lord, when I
    open your graves, and raise you from your
    graves, O my people.
And I will put my Spirit within you, and you
    shall live . . . (Ezekiel 37:12-14)

Ascension

And ascended into heaven, and sits at the right hand of the Father

After his resurrection from the dead Jesus appeared to men for a period of forty days after which he **"was taken up into heaven, and sat down at the right hand of God."** (Mark 16:19; see also Luke 24:50 and Acts 1:9-11)

The ascension of Jesus Christ is the final act of his earthly mission of salvation. The Son of God comes **"down from heaven"** to do the work which the Father gives him to do; and having accomplished all things, he returns to the Father bearing for all eternity the wounded and glorified humanity which he has assumed. (See e.g. John 17)

The doctrinal meaning of the ascension is the glorification of human nature, the reunion of man with God. It is indeed, the very penetration of man into the inexhaustible depths of divinity.

We have seen already that **"the heavens"** is the symbolical expression in the Bible for the uncreated, inmaterial, divine "realm of God" as one saint of the Church has called it. To say that Jesus is **"exalted at the right hand of God"** as St. Peter preached in the first Christian sermon (Acts 2:33) means exactly this: that man has been restored to communion with God, to a union which is, according to Orthodox doctrine, far greater and more perfect than that given to man in his original creation. (See Ephesians 1-2)

Man was created with the potential to be a **"partaker of the divine nature"**, to refer to the Apostle Peter once more. (II Peter 1:4) It is this participation in divinity, called **theosis** (which literally means deification or divinization) in Orthodox theology, that the ascension of Christ has fulfilled for humanity. The symbolical expression of the **"sitting at the right hand"** of God means nothing other than this. It does not mean that somewhere in the created universe the physical Jesus is sitting in a material throne.

The **Letter to the Hebrews** speaks of Christ's ascension in terms of the Jerusalem Temple. Just as the high

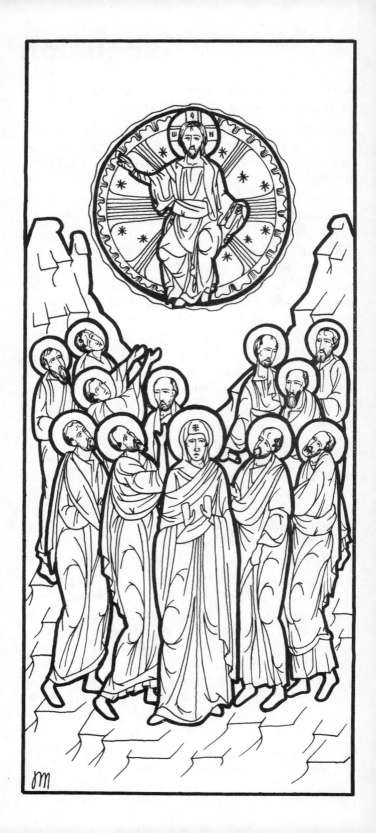

priests of Israel entered the "holy of holies" to offer sacrifice to God on behalf of themselves and the people, so Christ the one, eternal and perfect High Priest offers himself on the cross to God as the one eternal and perfect Sacrifice, not for himself but for all sinful men. As a man, Christ enters (once and for all) into the one eternal and perfect Holy of Holies: the very "Presence of God in the heavens".

> ...we have a great high priest who has passed through the heavens, Jesus, the Son of God.... (Hebrews 4:14)
>
> For it was fitting that we should have such a high priest, holy, blameless, unstained, separated from sinners, exalted above the heavens....He has no need like those high priests to offer sacrifice daily, first for his own sins and then for those of the people; he did this once and for all when he offered up himself.
>
> Now, the point in what we are saying is this: we have such a high priest, one who is seated at the right hand of the throne of the Majesty in heaven, a minister in the sanctuary and the true tabernacle which is set up not by man but by the Lord. (Hebrews 7:26; 8:2)
>
> For Christ has entered, not into a sanctuary made with hands, a copy of the true one, but into heaven itself, now to appear in the presence of God on our behalf. (Hebrews 9:24)
>
> ...when Christ had offered for all time a single sacrifice for sins, he sat down at the right hand of God, then to wait until his enemies should be made a stool for his feet. (Hebrews 10:12-13; Psalm 110:1)

Thus, the ascension of Christ is seen as man's first entry into that divine glorification for which he was originally created. The entry is made possible by the exaltation of the divine Son who emptied himself in human flesh in perfect self-offering to God.

Judgment

And He will come again with glory
to judge the living and the dead

> This Jesus who was taken up from you into heaven, will come the same way as you saw him go into heaven. (Acts 1:11)

These words of the angels are addressed to the apostles at the ascension of the Lord. Christ will come again in glory, "not to deal with sin, but to save those who are eagerly waiting for him." (Hebrews 9:28)

> For the Lord himself will descend from heaven with a cry of command, with the archangels' call, and with the sound of the trumpet of God. And the dead in Christ will rise first; then we who are alive, who are left, shall be caught up in the clouds to meet the Lord in the air, and so we shall always be with the Lord. (I Thessalonians 4:16-17, The Epistle Reading of the Orthodox Funeral Service)

The coming of the Lord at the end of the ages will be the **Day of Judgment**, the **Day of the Lord** foretold in the Old Testament and predicted by Jesus himself. (e.g. Daniel 7; Matthew 24) The exact time of the end is not foretold, not even by Jesus, so that men would always be prepared by constant vigil and good works.

The very presence of Christ as the Truth and the Light is itself the judgment of the world. In this sense all men and the whole world are already judged or, more accurately, already live in the full presence of that reality--Christ and his works--by which they will be ultimately judged. With Christ now revealed, there is no longer any excuse for ignorance and sin. (John 9:39)

At this point it is necessary to note that at the final judgment there will be those "on the left hand" who will go into "the eternal fire prepared for the devil and his angels." (Matthew 25:41; Revelation 20) That this is the case is no fault of God's. It is the fault only of men, for "as I hear, I judge and my judgment is just," says the Lord. (John 5:30)

God takes no "**pleasure in the death of the wicked.**" (**Ezekiel 18:22**) He "**desires all men to be saved and to come to the knowledge of the Truth.**" (**I Timothy 2:4**) He does everything in His power so that salvation and eternal life would be available and possible for all. There is nothing more that God can do. Everything now depends on man. If some men refuse the gift of life in communion with God, the Lord can only honor this refusal and respect the freedom of His creatures which He Himself has given and will not take back. God allows men to live "**with the devil and his angels**" if they so desire. Even in this He is loving and just. For if God's presence as the "**consuming fire**" (**Hebrews 12:29**) and the "**unapproachable light**" (**I Timothy 6:16**) which delights those who love Him only produces hatred and anguish in those who do not "**love His appearing**" (**II Timothy 4:8**), there is nothing that God can do except either to destroy His sinful creatures completely, or to destroy Himself. But God will exist and will allow His creatures to exist. He also will not hide His Face forever.

The doctrine of eternal hell, therefore, does not mean that God actively tortures people by some unloving and perverse means. It does not mean that God takes delight in the punishment and pain of His people whom He loves. Neither does it mean that God "separates Himself" from His people, thus causing them anguish in this separation (for indeed if people hate God, separation would be welcome, and not abhorred!). It means rather that God continues to allow all people, saints and sinners alike, to exist forever. All are raised from the dead into everlasting life: "**those who have done good, to the resurrection of judgment.**" (**John 5:29**) In the end, God will be "**all and in all.**" (**1 Corinthians 15:28**) For those who love God, resurrection from the dead and the presence of God will be paradise. For those who hate God, resurrection from the dead and the presence of God will be hell. This is the teaching of the fathers of the Church.

There is sprung up a light for the righteous, and its partner is joyful gladness. And the light of the righteous is everlasting . . .

One light alone let us shun — that which is the offspring of the sorrowful fire . . .

For I know a cleansing fire which Christ came to send upon the earth, and He Himself is called a Fire. This Fire takes away whatsoever is material and of evil quality; and this He desires to kindle with all speed . . .

I know also a fire which is not cleansing, but avenging . . . which He pours down on all sinners . . . that which is prepared for the devil and his angels . . . that which proceeds from the Face of the Lord and shall burn up His enemies round about . . . the unquenchable fire which . . . is eternal for the wicked. For all these belong to the destroying power, though some may prefer even in this place to take a more merciful view of this fire, worthily of Him who chastizes. (St. Gregory the Theologian)

. . . those who find themselves in Gehenna will be chastized with the scourge of love. How cruel and bitter this torment of love will be! For those who understand that they have sinned against love undergo greater sufferings than those produced of the most fearful tortures. The sorrow which takes hold of the heart which has sinned against love is more piercing than any other pain. It is not right to say that sinners in hell are deprived of the love of God . . . But love acts in two different ways, as suffering in the reproved, and as joy in the blessed. (St. Isaac of Syria)

Thus, man's final judgment and eternal destiny depends solely on whether or not man loves God and his brethren. It depends on whether or not man loves the light more than the darkness — or the darkness more than the light. It depends, we might say, on whether or not man loves Love and Light Itself; whether or not man loves Life — which is God Himself; the God revealed in creation, in all things, in the **"least of the brethren."**

The conditions of the final judgment are already known. Christ has given them Himself with absolute clarity.

> When the Son of Man shall come in His glory, and all the angels with Him, then He will sit on His glorious throne. Before Him will be gathered all the nations and He will separate them one from another as a shepherd separates the sheep from the goats, and He will place the sheep at His right hand, but the goats at the left. Then the King will say to those at His right hand, "Come, O blessed of my Father, inherit the kingdom prepared for you from the foundation of the world; for I was hungry and you gave me food, I was thirsty and you gave me drink, I was a stranger and you welcomed me, I was naked and you clothed me, I was sick and you visited me, I was in prison and you came to me."

> Then the righteous will answer Him, "Lord, when did we see Thee hungry and feed Thee, or thirsty and give Thee drink? And when did we see Thee a stranger and welcome Thee, or naked and clothe Thee? And when did we see Thee sick or in prison and visit Thee?"

> And the King will answer them, "Truly, I say to you, as you did it to one of the least of these my brethren, you did it to me."

> Then He will say to those at His left hand, "Depart from me, you cursed, into the eternal fire prepared for the devil and his angels; for I was hungry and you gave me no food, I was thirsty and you gave me no drink, I was a stranger and you did not welcome me, naked and you did not

clothe me, sick and in prison and you did not visit me."

Then they also will answer, "Lord, when did we see Thee hungry or thirsty or a stranger or naked or sick or in prison, and did not minister to Thee?"

Then He will answer them, "Truly, I say to you, as you did it not to one of the least of these, you did it not to me." And they will go away into eternal punishment, but the righteous into eternal life. (Matthew 25:31-46; Gospel Reading for Meatfare Sunday)

It is Christ who will judge, not God the Father. Christ has received the power of judgment "because He is the Son of Man." (John 5:27) Thus, man and the world are not judged by God "sitting on a cloud," as it were, but by One who is truly a man, the One who has suffered every temptation of this world and has emerged victorious. The world is judged by Him who was Himself hungry, thirsty, a stranger, naked, in prison, wounded, and yet the salvation of all. As the Crucified One, Christ has justly achieved the authority to make judgment for He alone has been the perfectly obedient servant of the Father who knows the depths of human tragedy by His own experience.

For He will render to every man according to his works: to those who by patience in well-doing seek for glory and honor and immortality, He will give eternal life; but for those who are factious and do not obey the truth, but obey wickedness, there will be wrath and fury. There will be tribulation and distress for every human being who does evil . . . but glory and honor and peace for every one who does good . . . for God shows no partiality. All who have sinned without the law, and all who have sinned under the law will be judged by the law. For it is not the hearers of the law who are righteous before God, but the doers of the law who will be justified. (Romans 2:6 ff.)

115

Kingdom of God

And of his kingdom there will be no end

Jesus is the royal Son of David, of whom it was prophesied by the angel at his birth:

> He will be great, and will be called the Son of the Most High; and the Lord will give to him the throne of his father David, and he will reign over the house of Jacob forever; and of his kingdom there will be no end. (Luke 1:32-33)

Through his sufferings as the Christ, Jesus achieved everlasting kingship and lordship over all creation. He has become "**King of kings and Lord of lords,**" sharing this title with God the Father Himself. (Deuteronomy 10:17; Daniel 2:47; Revelation 19:16) As a man, Jesus Christ is King of the Kingdom of God.

Christ came for no other reason than to bring God's kingdom to men. His very first public words are exactly those of his forerunner, John the Baptist: **Repent for the kingdom of heaven is at hand (Matthew 3:2, 4:17).**

All through his life Jesus spoke of the kingdom. In the sermons such as the Sermon on the Mount and the many parables, he told of the everlasting kingdom.

> **Blessed are the poor in spirit for theirs is the kingdom of heaven...**

> **Blessed are they who are persecuted for righteousness sake for theirs is the kingdom of heaven.**

> **He who does these commandments and teaches them shall be called great in the kingdom of heaven.**

> **But seek ye first the kingdom of heaven and its righteousness, and all things will be yours as well.**

> **Not everyone who says to me, "Lord, Lord," shall enter the kingdom of heaven, but he who does the will of my Father who is in heaven. (Matthew 5-7)**

The mustard seed, the leaven, the pearl of great price, the lost coin, the treasure in the field, the fishing net, the wedding feast, the banquet, the house of the Father, the vineyard . . . all are signs of the kingdom which Jesus has come to bring. And on the night of His last supper with the disciples He tells the apostles openly:

> **You are those who have continued with me in my trials; as my Father appointed a kingdom for me, so do I appoint for you that you may eat and drink at my table in my kingdom, and sit on thrones judging the twelve tribes of Israel. (Luke 22:28-30; Reading of the Vigil of Holy Thursday)**

Christ's kingdom is "not of this world." (John 18:31) He says this to Pontius Pilate when being mocked as king, revealing in this humiliation His genuine divine kingship. The Kingdom of God, which Christ will rule, will come with power at the end of time when the Lord will fill all creation and will be truly "**all, and in all.**" (**Colossians 3:11**) The Church, which in popular Orthodox doctrine is called the Kingdom of God on earth, has already mysteriously been given this experience. In the Church, Christ is already acknowledged, glorified and served as the only king and lord; and His Holy Spirit, whom the saints of the Church have identified with the Kingdom of God, is already given to the world in the Church with full graciousness and power.

The Kingdom of God, therefore, is a Divine Reality. It is the reality of God's presence among men through Christ and the Holy Spirit. "**For the Kingdom of God . . . means . . . peace and joy and righteousness in the Holy Spirit.**" (**Romans 14:17**) The Kingdom of God as a spiritual, divine reality is given to men by Christ in the Church. It is celebrated and participated in the sacramental mysteries of the faith. It is witnessed to in the scriptures, the councils, the canons and the saints. It will become the universal, final cosmic reality for the whole of creation at the end of the ages when Christ comes in glory to fill all things with Himself by the Holy Spirit, that God might be "**all and in all.**" (**I Corinthians 15:28**)

Holy Spirit

And in the Holy Spirit, Lord and Giver of Life, who proceeds from the Father, who together with the Father and the Son is worshipped and glorified, who spoke by the prophets

The Holy Spirit bears the title of **Lord** with God the Father and Christ the Son. He is the Spirit of God and Spirit of Christ. He is eternal, uncreated and divine; always existing with the Father and the Son; perpetually worshipped and glorified with them in the oneness of the Holy Trinity.

Just like the Son, there was no time when there was no Holy Spirit. The Spirit is before creation. He comes forth from God, as does the Son, in a timeless, eternal **procession. "He proceeds from the Father"**, in eternity in a divinely instantaneous and perpetual movement. (John 15:26)

Orthodox doctrine confesses that God the Father is the eternal origin and source of the Spirit, just as He is the source of the Son. Yet, the Church affirms as well that the manner of the Father's possession and production of the Spirit and the Son differ according to the difference between the Son being "born", and the Spirit "proceeding." There have been many attempts by holy men inspired by God and with a genuine experience of His Trinitarian life to explain the distinction between the procession of the Spirit and the begetting or generation of the Son. For us it is enough to see that the difference between the two lies in the distinction between the divine persons and actions of the Son and the Spirit in relation to the Father, and so as well to each other and to the world. It is necessary to note further that all words and concepts about God and divinity, including those of "procession" and "generation" must give way before the mystical vision of the actual Divine Reality which they express. God may somehow be grasped by men as He has chosen to reveal Himself. However, the essence of His Triune existence remains—and will always remain—essentially inconceivable and inexpressible to created minds and lips. This does not mean that words about God are meaningless. It only means that they are inadequate to the Reality which they seek to express.

At this point also it is necessary to note that the Roman and Protestant churches differ in their credal statement about God by adding that the Holy Spirit proceeds from the Father "and the Son" **(filioque)**—a doctrinal addition unacceptable to Orthodoxy since it is both unscriptural and inconsistent with the Orthodox vision of God.

With the affirmation of the divinity of the Holy Spirit, and the necessity of worshipping and glorifying him with the Father and the Son, the Orthodox Church affirms that the Divine Reality, called also the **Deity** or the **Godhead** in the Orthodox Tradition, is the **Holy Trinity**. (see Section III)

The Holy Spirit is essentially one in his eternal existence with the Father and the Son; and so, in every action of God toward the world, the Holy Spirit is necessarily acting. Thus, in the **Genesis** account of creation it is written: **"The Spirit of God was moving over the face of the waters." (Genesis 1:2)** It is this same Spirit who is the **"breath of life"** for all living things and particularly for man, made in the image and likeness of God. (Genesis 1:30; 2:7) Generally speaking the Spirit in Hebrew is called the "breath" or the "wind" of Yahweh. It is he who makes everything alive, the **"giver of life"** who upholds and sustains the universe in its existence and life. (e.g. Psalm 104:29; Job 33:4)

The Holy Spirit is also he who inspires the saints to speak God's word and to do God's will. He anoints the prophets, priests and kings of the Old Testament; and **"in the fullness of time"** it is this same Spirit who **"descends and remains"** on Jesus of Nazareth, making him the Messiah (anointed) of God and manifesting him as such to the world. Thus, in the New Testament at the first **epiphany** (which means literally showing forth or manifestation) of Christ as the Messiah—his baptism by John in the Jordan—the Holy Spirit is revealed as descending and resting upon him **"as a**

119

dove from heaven." (John 1:32; Luke 3:22. See also Matthew 3:16 and Mark 1:9) It is important to note, both here and in the account of the Spirit's coming on the Day of Pentecost, as well as in other places in the Scriptures, that the words "as" and "like" are used in order to avoid an incorrect "physical" interpretation of the events recorded where the Bible itself is literally speaking in quite a symbolical and metaphorical way.

Jesus begins his public work after his baptism, and immediately refers Isaiah's prophecy about the Messiah directly to himself: **"The Spirit of the Lord is upon me..."** (Isaiah 61:1; Luke 4:18)

All the days of his life Jesus is **"full of the Holy Spirit"**—preaching, teaching, healing, casting out devils and accomplishing every sign and wonder of his messiahship by the Spirit's power. (Luke 4:11) It is written that even his self-offering to God on the cross is made **"through the eternal Spirit"** (Hebrews 9:4) And it is through the same divine Spirit that he and all men with him are risen from the dead. (Ezekiel 37:1-4)

On the day of Pentecost the Holy Spirit comes upon the disciples of Christ in the form of **"tongues as of fire,"** with the sound **"like that of a mighty rushing wind."** (Acts 2:1-4) We note once more the use of "as" and "like". The coming of the Spirit on Pentecost is the final fulfillment of Christ's earthly messianic mission, the beginning of the Christian Church. It is the fulfillment of the Old Testamental prophecy that in the time of the messiah-king, the Spirit of God will be **"poured out on all flesh."** (Joel 2:28; Acts 1:14) It is the condition of the age of the final and everlasting covenant of perfect mercy and peace. (Ezekiel 34: 37; Jeremiah 31-33; Isaiah 11: 42, 44, 61)

The Christian Church lives by the Holy Spirit. The Spirit alone is the guarantee of God's Kingdom on earth. He is the sole guarantee that God's life and

120

truth and love are with men. Only by the Holy Spirit can man and the world fulfill that for which they were created by God. All of God's actions toward man and the world—in creation, salvation and final glorification—are from the Father through the Son (Word) in the Holy Spirit; and all of man's capabilities of response to God are in the same Spirit, through the same Son to the same Father.

The Holy Spirit is the Spirit of life.

If the Spirit of him who raised Jesus from the dead dwells in you, he who raised Jesus from the dead will give life to your mortal bodies through the Spirit who dwells in you. (Romans 8:11)

The Holy Spirit is the Spirit of truth.

When the Spirit of Truth comes he will guide you into all the Truth; for he will not speak on his own authority, but whatever he hears he will speak, and he will declare to you the things that are to come. (John 16:13; see also John 14:25; John 15:26)

The Holy Spirit is the Spirit of divine sonship.

For all who are led by the Spirit are sons of God. For you did not receive the Spirit of slavery.... but you received the Spirit of sonship. When we cry "Abba! Father!" it is the Spirit himself bearing witness with our spirit that we are children of God. (Romans 8:14; also Galations 4:6)

The Holy Spirit is the personal presence of the new and everlasting covenant between God and man, the seal and guarantee of the Kingdom of God, the power of the divine indwelling of God in man.

...you are a letter from Christ, delivered by us, written not with ink but with the Spirit of the living God, not on tablets of stone but on tablets of human hearts....our sufficiency is from God

121

who has qualified us to be ministers of a new covenant, not in written code but in the Spirit, for the written code kills, but the Spirit gives life. (II Corinthians 3:2-6)

Do you not know that you are God's temple and that God's Spirit dwells in you....For God's temple is holy, and that temple you are. (I Corinthians 3:16; also Romans 6:19)

...through him (Christ) we both have access in one Spirit to the Father. So then you are no longer strangers and sojourners but you are fellow citizens with the saints and members of the household of God, built upon the foundation of apostles and the prophets, Christ Jesus himself being the cornerstone, in whom the whole structure is joined together and grows in a holy temple in the Lord; in whom you also are built into it for a dwelling place of God in the Spirit. (Ephesians 2:18-22; also I Peter 2:4-9)

In the Holy Spirit men have the possibility of receiving every gift from God, of sharing His divine nature and life, of doing what Christ has done by fulfilling his "new commandment" to love one another even as he has loved us, "because God's love has been poured into our hearts through the Holy Spirit which he has given us." (Romans 5:5)

The fruit of the Spirit is love, joy, peace, patience, kindness, goodness, faithfulness, gentleness, self-control....And those who belong to Christ Jesus have crucified the flesh with its passions and desires. If we live by the Spirit...he who sows to the Spirit will from the Spirit reap eternal life. (Galatians 5:22-25; 6:8)

Church

In one, holy, catholic and apostolic Church

Church as a word means those called as a particular people to perform a particular task. The Christian Church is the assembly of God's chosen people called to keep his word and to do his will and his work in the world and in the heavenly kingdom.

In the Scriptures the Church is called the Body of Christ (Romans 12; I Corinthians 10, 12; Colossians 1) and the Bride of Christ (Ephesians 5; Revelation 21). It is likened as well to God's living Temple. (Ephesians 2; I Peter 2) and is called "the pillar and bulwark of Truth." (I Timothy 3:15)

One Church

The Church is **one** because God is one, and because Christ and the Holy Spirit are one. There can only be one Church and not many. And this one Church, because its unity depends on God, Christ and the Spirit, may never be broken. Thus, according to Orthodox doctrine, the Church is indivisible; men may be in it or out of it, but they may not divide it.

According to Orthodox teaching, the unity of the Church is man's free unity in the truth and love of God. Such unity is not brought about or established by any human authority or juridical power, but by God alone. To the extent that men are in the truth and love of God, they are members of His Church.

Orthodox Christians believe that in the historical Orthodox Church there exists the full possibility of participating totally in the Church of God, and that only sins and false human choices (heresies) put men outside of this unity. In non-Orthodox Christian groups the Orthodox claim that there are certain formal obstacles, varying in different groups, which, if accepted and followed by men, will prevent their perfect unity with God and will thus destroy the genuine unity of the Church. (e.g. the papacy in the Roman Church)

Within the unity of the Church man is what he is created to be and can grow for eternity in divine life in communion with God through Christ in the Holy Spirit. The unity of the Church is not broken by time or space and is not limited merely to those alive upon the earth. The unity of the Church is the unity of the Blessed Trinity and of all of those who live with God: the holy angels, the righteous dead, and those who live upon the earth according to the commandments of Christ and the power of the Holy Spirit.

Holy Church

The Church is **holy** because God is holy, and because Christ and the Holy Spirit are holy. The holiness of the Church comes from God. The members of the Church are holy to the extent that they live in communion with God.

Within the earthly Church, people participate in God's holiness. Sin and error separate them from this divine holiness as it does from the divine unity. Thus, the earthly members and institutions of the Church cannot be identified as such with the Church as holy.

The faith and life of the Church on earth is expressed in its doctrines, sacraments, scriptures, services and saints which maintain the Church's essential unity, and which can certainly be affirmed as "holy" because of God's presence and action in them.

Catholic Church

The Church is also catholic because of its relation to God, Christ, and the Holy Spirit. The word **catholic** means full, complete, whole, with nothing lacking. God alone is full and total reality; in God alone is there nothing lacking.

Sometimes the catholicity of the Church is understood in terms of the Church's universality through-

out time and space. While it is true that the Church is universal—for all men at all times and in all places—this universality is not the real meaning of the term "catholic" when it is used to define the Church. The term "catholic" as originally used to define the Church (as early as the first decades of the second century) was a definition of quality rather than quantity. Calling the Church **catholic** means to define **how** it is, namely, full and complete, all-embracing, and with nothing lacking.

Even before the Church was spread over the world, it was defined as catholic. The original Jerusalem Church of the apostles, or the early city-churches of Antioch, Ephesus, Corinth, or Rome, were catholic. These churches were catholic—as is each and every Orthodox church today--because nothing essential was lacking for them to be the genuine Church of Christ. God Himself is fully revealed and present in each church through Christ and the Holy Spirit, acting in the local community of believers with its apostolic doctrine, ministry (hierarchy) and sacraments, thus requiring nothing to be added to it in order for it to participate fully in the Kingdom of God.

To believe in the Church as catholic, therefore, is to express the conviction that the fullness of God is present in the Church and that nothing of the "abundant life" that Christ gives to the world in the Spirit is lacking to it. (John 10:10) It is to confess exactly that the Church is indeed "**the fullness of him who fills all in all.**" (Ephesians 1:23; also Colossians 2:10)

Apostolic Church

The word **apostolic** describes that which has a mission, that which has "been sent" to accomplish a task.

Christ and the Holy Spirit are both "apostolic" because both have been sent by the Father to the World. It is not only repeated in the Scripture on numerous occasions how Christ has been sent by the Father, and the Spirit sent through Christ from the Father, but it also has been recorded explicitly that Christ is "**the apostle...of our confession.**" (Hebrews 3:1)

As Christ was sent from God, so Christ Himself chose and sent His apostles. "**As the Father has sent me, even so I send you...receive ye the Holy Spirit**", the risen Christ says to His disciples. Thus, the apostles go out to the world, becoming the first foundation of the Christian Church.

In this sense, then, the Church is called apostolic: first, as it is built upon Christ and the Holy Spirit sent from God and upon those apostles who were sent by Christ, filled with the Holy Spirit; and secondly, as the Church in its earthly members is itself sent by God to bear witness to His Kingdom, to keep His word and to do His will and His works in this world.

Orthodox Christians believe in the Church as they believe in God and Christ and the Holy Spirit. Faith in the Church is part of the creedal statement of Christian believers. The Church is herself an object of faith as the divine reality of the Kingdom of God given to men by Christ and the Holy Spirit; the divine community founded by Christ against which "**the gates of hell shall not prevail.**" (Matthew 16:18)

The Church, and faith in the Church, is an essential element of Christian doctrine and life. Without the Church as a divine, mystical, sacramental and spiritual reality in the midst of the fallen and sinful world there can be no full and perfect communion with God. The Church is God's gift to the world. It is the gift of salvation, of knowledge and enlightenment, of the forgiveness of sins, of the victory over darkness and death. It is the gift of communion with God through Christ and the Holy Spirit. This gift is given totally, once and for all, with no reservations on God's part. It remains forever, until the close of the ages: invincible and indestructible. Men may sin and fight against the Church, believers may fall away and be separated

127

from the Church, but the Church itself, the **"pillar and bulwark of the truth"** (1 Timothy 3:15) remains forever.

. . . (God) **has put all things under His** (Christ's) **feet and has made Him the head over all things for the Church, which is His body, the fullness of Him who fills all in all.**

. . . **for through Him we . . . have access in one Spirit to the Father. So then you are no longer strangers and sojourners, but you are fellow-citizens with the saints and members of the household of God, built upon the foundation of the apostles and prophets, Christ Jesus Himself being the cornerstone, in whom the whole struc-ture is joined together and grows into a holy temple in the Lord; in whom you also are built into it for a dwelling place of God in the Spirit.**

. . . **Christ loved the Church and gave Himself up for her, that he might sanctify her by the wash-ing of water with the word, that He might pre-sent the Church to Himself in splendor, without spot or wrinkle or any such thing, that she might be holy and without blemish . . . This is a Great Mystery . . . Christ and the Church . . . (Ephe-sians 1:21-23; 2:19-22; 5:25-32)**

Sacraments

I confess one baptism
for the remission of sins

The way of entry into the Christian Church is by baptism in the name of the Father and of the Son and of the Holy Spirit. (Matthew 28:19, the Baptismal Gospel Reading in the Orthodox Church)

Baptism as a word means immersion or submersion in water. It was practiced in the Old Testament and even in some pagan religions as the sign of death and rebirth. Thus, John the Baptist was baptizing as the sign of new life and **repentance** which means literally a change of mind, and so of desires and actions in preparation of the coming of the Kingdom of God in Christ.

In the Church, the meaning of **baptism** is death and rebirth in Christ. It is the personal experience of Easter given to each man, the real possibility to die and to be **"born anew"**. (John 3:3)

> Do you not know that all of us who have been baptized into Christ Jesus were baptized into his death? We were buried therefore with him by baptism into death, so that as Christ was raised from the dead by the glory of the Father, we too might walk in newness of life. For if we have been united with him in a death like his, we shall certainly be united with him in a resurrection like his. (Romans 6:3-5; Baptismal Epistle Reading in the Orthodox Church; See also Colossians 2:12; 3:1)

The baptismal experience is the fundamental Christian experience, the primary condition for the whole of Christian life. Everything in the Church has its origin and context in baptism for everything in the Church originates and lives by the resurrection of Christ. Thus, following baptism comes "the seal of the gift of the Holy Spirit," the mystery (sacrament) of chrismation which is man's personal experience of Pentecost. And the completion and fulfillment of these fundamental Christian mysteries comes in the mystery of Holy Communion with God in the divine liturgy of the Church.

Only persons who are committed to Christ in the Orthodox Church through baptism and chrismation may offer and receive the holy eucharist in the Orthodox Church. The holy eucharist is Holy Communion. As such it is not just a "means of sanctification" for individual believers, a means through which private persons gain "communion" with God according to their own private consciences, beliefs and practices. It is rather the all-embracing act of Holy Communion of many persons having the same faith, the same hope, the same baptism. It is the corporate act of many persons having one mind, one heart, one mouth in the service of the one God and Lord, in the one Christ and the one Holy Spirit.

To participate in Holy Communion in the Orthodox Church is to identify oneself fully with all of the members of the Orthodox faith, living and dead; and to identify oneself fully with every aspect of the Orthodox Church: its history, councils, canons, dogmas, disciplines. It is to "take on oneself" the direct and concrete responsibility for everyone and everything connected in and with the Orthodox tradition and to profess responsibility for the everyday life of the Orthodox Church. It is to say before God and men that one is willing to be judged, in time and eternity, for what the Orthodox Church is and for what the Orthodox Church stands for in the midst of the earth.

Entering into the "Holy Communion" of the Orthodox Church through baptism and chrismation, one lives according to the life of the Church in every possible way. One is first of all faithful to the doctrine and discipline of the Church by faithful communion with the hierarchy of the Church who are those members of the Body sacramentally responsible for the teachings and practices of the Church; the sacramental images of the Church's identity and continuity in all places and

all times. When one enters into the community of marriage, a union of one man and one woman forever according to the teaching of Jesus Christ, this union is sanctified and made eternal and divine in the sacramental mystery of matrimony in the Church. When one is sick and suffering, he "calls for the priests of the Church" to "pray over him, anointing him with oil" in the sacramental mystery of holy unction. (Cf. James 5:4) When one sins and falls away from the life of the Church, one returns to the "Holy Communion" of the divine community by the sacramental mystery of confession and repentance. And when one dies, he is returned to his Creator in the midst of the Church, with the prayers and intercessions of the faithful brothers and sisters in Christ and the Spirit. Thus the entire life of the person is lived in and with the Church as the life of fullness and newness in God Himself, the Church which is the mystical presence of God's Kingdom which is not of this world. (See Book II, *Worship*)

The confession of "one baptism for the remission of sins," therefore, is the confession of the total newness of life given to men in the Church because Christ is risen.

> **If then you have been raised with Christ, seek the things that are above, where Christ is, seated at the right hand of God. Set your minds on things that are above, not on things that are on earth. For you have died and your life is hid with Christ in God. When Christ who is our life appears, then you also will appear with Him in glory. (Colossians 3:1-4)**

Thus, in the Church, the whole of life is the one which begins in the new birth of baptism, the "life hid with Christ in God." All of the mysteries of the Christian faith are contained in this new life. Everything in the Church flows out of the waters of baptism: the remission of sins and life eternal.

Eternal Life

**I look for the resurrection of the dead
and the life of the world (ages) to come**

The Orthodox Church does not believe merely in the immortality of the soul, and in the goodness and ultimate salvation of only spiritual reality. Following the Scriptures, Orthodox Christians believe in the goodness of the human body and of all material and physical creation. Thus, in its faith in resurrection and eternal life, the Orthodox Church looks not to some "other world" for salvation, but to this very world so loved by God, resurrected and glorified by Him, filled with His own divine presence.

At the end of the ages God will reveal His presence and will fill all creation with Himself. For those who love Him it will be paradise. For those who hate Him it will be hell. And all physical creation, together with the righteous, will rejoice and be glad in His coming.

> The wilderness and the solitary places will be glad; the desert shall rejoice and blossom in abundance. (Isaiah 35:1)

> For behold I create new heavens and a new earth says the Lord, and the former things shall not be remembered or come to mind. But be glad and rejoice forever in that which I create, for behold I create Jerusalem a rejoicing and her people a joy. (Isaiah 65: 17-18)

The visions of the prophets and those of the Christian apostles about things to come are one and the same:

> Then I saw a new heaven and a new earth: for the first heaven and the first earth had passed away, and the sea was no more. And I saw the holy city, new Jerusalem, coming down out of heaven from God, prepared as a bride adorned for her husband; and I heard a great voice from the throne saying, "Behold, the dwelling of God is with men. He will dwell with them, and they shall be his people, and God himself will be with them; he will wipe away every tear from their eyes, and death shall be no more, neither shall there be

133

mourning nor crying nor pain any more, for the former things have passed away." (Revelation 21:1-5)

When the Kingdom of God fills all creation, all things will be made new. This world will again be that paradise for which it was originally created. This is the Orthodox doctrine of the final fate of man and his universe.

It is sometimes argued, however, that this world will be totally destroyed and that God will create everything new "out of nothing" by the act of a second creation. Those who hold this opinion appeal to such texts as that found in the second letter of Saint Peter:

But the day of the Lord will come like a thief, and then the heavens will pass away...and the elements will be dissolved with fire, and the earth and the works that are upon it will be burned up. (II Peter 3:10)

Because the Bible never speaks about a "second creation" and because it continually and consistently witnesses that God loves the world which He has made and does everything that He can to save it, the Orthodox Tradition never interprets such scriptural texts as teaching the actual annihilation of creation by God. It understands such texts as speaking metaphorically of the great catastrophe which creation must endure, including even the righteous, in order for it to be cleansed, purified, made perfect and saved. It teaches as well that there is an "eternal fire" for the ungodly, an eternal condition of their being destroyed. But in any case the "trial by fire" which "destroys the ungodly" is in no way understood by the Orthodox in the sense that creation is doomed to total destruction, despised by the loving Lord who created it and called it "very good". (Genesis 1:31; also I Corinthians 3: 13-15; Hebrews 12:25-29; Isaiah 66; Revelation 20-22)

3

THE HOLY TRINITY

Holy Trinity

The doctrine of the Holy Trinity is not merely an "article of faith" which men are called to "believe." It is not simply a dogma which the Church requires its good members to "accept on faith." Neither is the doctrine of the Holy Trinity the invention of scholars and academicians, the result of intellectual speculation and philosophical thinking.

The doctrine of the Holy Trinity arises from man's deepest experiences with God. It comes from the genuine living knowledge of those who have come to know God in faith.

The paragraphs which follow are intended to show something of what God has revealed of Himself to the saints of the Church. To grasp the words and concepts of the doctrine of the Trinity is one thing; to know the Living Reality of God behind these words and concepts is something else. We must work and pray so that we might pass beyond every word and concept about God and to come to know Him for ourselves in our own living union with Him: **"The Father through the Son in the Holy Spirit."** (Ephesians 2: 18-22)

The Holy Trinity Revealed

In the Old Testament we find Yahweh, the one Lord and God, acting toward the world through His Word and His Spirit. In the New Testament the **"Word becomes flesh."** (**John 1:14**) As Jesus of Nazareth, the only-begotten Son of God becomes man. And the Holy Spirit, who is in Jesus making him the Christ, is poured forth from God upon all flesh. (Acts 2:17)

One cannot read the Bible nor the history of the Church without being struck by the numerous references to God the Father, the Son (Word) of God and the Holy Spirit. The New Testament record, and the life of the Orthodox Church is absolutely incomprehensible and meaningless without constant affirmation of the existence, interrelation and interaction of the Father, the Son and the Holy Spirit towards each other and towards man and the world.

Wrong Doctrines of the Trinity

The main question for the Church to answer about God is that of the relationship between the Father, the Son and the Holy Spirit. According to Orthodox Tradition, there are a number of wrong doctrines which must be rejected.

One wrong doctrine is that the Father alone is God and that the Son and the Holy Spirit are creatures, made "from nothing" like angels, men and the world. The Church answers that the Son and the Holy Spirit are not creatures, but are uncreated and divine with the Father, and they act with the Father in the divine act of creation of all that exists.

Another wrong doctrine is that God in Himself is One God who merely appears in different forms to the world: Now as the Father, then as the Son, and still again as the Holy Spirit. The Church answers once more that the Son and Word is "in the beginning with God" (John 1:12) as is the Holy Spirit, and that the Three are eternally distinct. The Son is "of God" and the Spirit is "of God." The Son and the Spirit are not merely aspects of God, without, so to speak, a life and existence of their own. How strange it would be to imagine, for example, that when the Son becomes man and prays to his Father and acts in obedience to Him, it is all an illusion with no reality in fact, a sort of divine presentation played before the world with no reason or truth for it at all!

A third wrong doctrine is that God is one, and that the Son and the Spirit are merely names for relations which God has with Himself. Thus, the Thought and Speech of God is called the Son, while the Life and Action of God is called the Spirit; but in fact—in genuine actuality—there are no such "realities in themselves" as the Son of God and the Spirit of God. Both are just metaphors for mere aspects of God. Again, however, in such a doctrine the Son and the Spirit have no existence and no life of their own. They are not real, but are mere illusions.

Still another wrong doctrine is that the Father is one God, the Son is another God, and the Holy Spirit still another God. There cannot be "three gods," says the Church, and certainly not "gods" who are created or made. Still less can there be "three gods" of whom the Father is "higher" and the others "lower". For there to be more than one God, or "degrees of divinity" are both contradictions which cannot be defended, either by divine revelation or by logical thinking.

Thus, the Church teaches that while there is only One God, yet there are Three who are God--the Father, the Son, and the Holy Spirit—perfectly united and never divided yet not merged into one with no proper distinction. How then does the Church defend its doctrine that God is both One and yet Three?

One God, One Father

First of all, it is the Church's teaching and its deepest experience that there is only one God because there is only one Father.

In the Bible the term "God" with very few exceptions is used primarily as a name for the Father. Thus, the Son is the "Son of God," and the Spirit is the "Spirit of God." The Son is born from the Father, and the Spirit proceeds from the Father—both in the same timeless and eternal action of the Father's own being.

In this view, the Son and the Spirit are both one with God and in no way separated from Him. Thus, the Divine Unity consists of the Father, with His Son and

His Spirit distinct from Himself and yet perfectly united together in Him.

One God: One Divine Nature and Being

What the Father is, the Son and the Spirit are also. This is the Church's teaching. The Son, born of the Father, and the Spirit, proceeding from Him, share the divine nature with God, being "of one essence" with Him.

Thus, as the Father is "ineffable, inconceivable, invisible, incomprehensible, ever-existing and eternally the same" (Divine Liturgy of St. John Chrysostom), so the Son and the Spirit are exactly the same. Every attribute of divinity which belongs to God the Father –life, love, wisdom, truth, blessedness, holiness, power, purity, joy--belongs equally as well to the Son and the Holy Spirit. The being, nature, essence, existence and life of God the Father, the Son and the Holy Spirit are absolutely and identically one and the same.

One God: One Divine Action and Will

Since the being of the Holy Trinity is one, whatever the Father wills, the Son and the Holy Spirit will also. What the Father does, the Son and the Holy Spirit do also. There is no will and no action of God the Father which is not at the same time the will and action of the Son and the Holy Spirit.

In Himself, in eternity, as well as towards the world in creation, revelation, incarnation, redemption, sanctification and glorification--the will and action of the Trinity are one: from the divine Father, through the divine Son, in the divine Holy Spirit. Every action of God is the action of the Three. No one person of the Trinity acts independently of or in isolation from the others. The action of each is the action of all; the action of all is the action of each. And the divine action is essentially one.

One God: One Divine Knowledge and Love

Since each person of the Trinity is one with the others, each knows the same Truth and exercises the same Love. The knowledge of each is the knowledge of all, and the Love of each is the Love of all.

If taken in distinction, each person of the Trinity knows and loves the others with such absolute perfection, knowledge and love that there is nothing unknown and nothing unloved of each in the others, and all in all. Thus, if the creaturely knowledge of men can unite minds in full unanimity, and if the creaturely love of men can bring the divided together into one heart and one soul and even one flesh, how incomparably more perfect and absolutely uniting must be the oneness when the Knowers and Lovers are eternal and divine.

The Three Divine Persons

In Orthodox terminology the Father, the Son and the Holy Spirit are called three divine **persons. Person** is defined here simply as the **subject of existence and life, hypostasis** in the traditional church language.

As the being, essence or nature of a reality answers the question "what?", the **person** of a reality answers the question "which one?" or "who?". Thus, when we ask "What is God?" we answer that God is the divine, perfect, eternal, absolute...And when we ask "Who is God?" we answer that God is the Father, the Son and the Holy Spirit.

The saints of the Church have explained this tri-unity of God by using such an example from worldly existence. We see three men. "What are they?" we ask. "They are human beings," we answer. Each is man, possessing the same humanity and the same human nature defined in a certain way: created, temporal, physical, rational, etc. In **what** they are, the three men are one. But in **who** they are, they are three, each absolutely unique and distinct from the others. Each man in his own unique way is distinctly a man. One

141

man is not the other, though each man is still human with one and the same human nature and form.

Turning to God, we may ask in the same way: "**What** is it?". In reply we say that it is God defined as absolute perfection: "ineffable, inconceivable, invisible, incomprehensible, ever-existing and eternally the same." We then ask, "**Who** is it?", and we answer that it is the Trinity: Father, Son and Holy Spirit.

In **who** God is, there are three persons who are each absolutely unique and distinct. Each is not the other, though each is still divine with the same divine nature and form. Therefore, while being one in **what** they are; the Father, the Son and the Holy Spirit are yet Three in **who** they are. And because of **what** and **who** they are—namely, uncreated, divine persons—they are undivided and perfectly united in their timeless, spaceless, sizeless, shapeless super-essential existence, as well as in their one divine life, knowledge, love, goodness, power, will, action, etc.

Thus, according to the Orthodox Tradition, it is the mystery of God that there are Three who are divine; Three who live and act by one and the same divine perfection, yet each according to his own personal distinctness and uniqueness. Thus it is said that the Father, the Son and the Holy Spirit are each divine with the same divinity, yet each in his own divine way. And as the uncreated divinity has three divine subjects, so each divine action has three divine actors; there are three divine aspects to every action of God, yet the action remains one and the same.

We discover, therefore, one God the Father Almighty with His one unique Son (Image and Word) and His one Holy Spirit. There is one living God with His one perfect divine Life, who is personally the Son, with His one Spirit of Life. There is one True God with His one divine Truth, who is personally the Son, with His one Spirit of Truth. There is one wise and loving God with His one Wisdom and Love, who is personally the Son, with His one Spirit of Wisdom and Love. The

142

examples could go on indefinitely: the one divine Father personifying every aspect of His divinity in His one divine Son, who is personally activated by His one divine Spirit. We will see the living implications of the Trinity as we survey the activity of God in his actions toward man and the world.

The Holy Trinity in Creation

God the Father created the world through the Son (Word) in the Holy Spirit. The Word of God is present in all that exists, making it to exist by the power of the Spirit. Thus, according to Orthodox doctrine, the universe itself is a revelation of God in the Word and the Spirit. The Word is in all that exists, causing it to be, and the Spirit is in all that exists as the power of its being and life.

This is most evident in God's special creature, man. Man is made in the image of God, and so he bears within him the unique likeness of God which is eternally and perfectly expressed in the divine Son of God, the Uncreated and Absolute Image of the Father. Thus, man is "logical"; that is, he participates in God's Logos (the Son and Word) and so is free, knowing, loving, reflecting on the creaturely level the very nature of God as the uncreated Son does on the level of divinity.

Man also is "spiritual"; he is the special temple of God's Spirit. The Breath of God's Life is breathed into him in the most special way. Thus, among creatures man alone is empowered to imitate God and to participate in His life. Man has the competence and ability to become a Son of God, mirroring the eternal Son, reflecting the divine nature because he is inspired by the Holy Spirit as is no other creature. Thus, one saint of the Church has said that for man to be a man, he must have the Spirit of God in him. Only then can he fulfill his humanity; only then can he be made a true Son of God, likened to him who is only-begotten.

143

On the most basic level of creation, therefore, we see the Trinitarian dimensions of the being and action of God: the Word and the Spirit of God enter man and the world to allow them to be and to become that for which the Father has willed their existence.

The Holy Trinity in Salvation

With man's failure to fulfill himself in his created uniqueness, God undertakes the special action of salvation. The Father sends forth His Son (Word) and His Spirit in yet another mission. The Word and the Spirit come to the Old Testament saints to make known the Father. The Word, as it were, incarnates himself in the Law (in Hebrew called the "words") which is inspired by the Spirit. The Spirit inspires the prophets to proclaim the Word of God. Thus, the Law and the Prophets are revelations of God in His Word and His Spirit. They are partial revelations, "shadows" (as the New Testament calls them), prefiguring the total revelation of the "fullness of time" and preparing its coming.

When the time is fulfilled and the world is made ready, the Word and the Spirit come once more--no longer by their mere action and power, but now in their own persons, dwelling personally in the world.

The Word becomes flesh. The only-begotten Son is born as a man, Jesus of Nazareth. And the Spirit who is in him is given to all men to make them also sons of the Father in an eternal development of attaining His perfection by growing forever "to the measure of the stature of the fullness of Christ." (Ephesians 4:13)

Thus, in the New Testament we have the full epiphany of God, the full manifestation of the Holy Trinity: the Father through the Son in the Spirit to us; and we in the Spirit through the Son to the Father.

144

The Holy Trinity in the Church

The life of the Church is the life of men in the Holy Trinity. In the Church all become one in Christ, all put on the deified humanity of the Son of God. "**For as many as have been baptized into Christ have put on Christ.**" (Galations 3:27) The unity of the Church is the unity of many into one, the one Body of Christ, the one living temple of God, the one people and family of God.

Within the one body there are many individual members. Many "living stones" constitute the living temple. Many brothers and sisters make up the one family of which God is the Father. The unique diversity of each member of the one Body of Christ is guaranteed by the presence of the Holy Spirit. Each unique person is inspired by the Spirit to be a true man, a true son of God in his own distinct way. Thus, as the Body of the Church is one in Christ, the one Holy Spirit gives to each member the possibility of fulfilling himself in God and so of being one with all others in calling God "Father" (See I Corinithians 12)

The Church, then, as the perfect unity of many persons into one fully united organism, is a reflection of the Trinity itself. For the Church, being many unique and distinct persons, is called to be one mind, one heart, one soul and one body in the one Truth and Love of God Himself. The calling of the Church to be one in all things is the prototype of the vocation of all mankind which was originally created by God as many persons in one nature, ultimately destined by God for ever-more-perfect growth in free unity of Truth and Love, in the life of God's Kingdom.

The Holy Trinity in the Sacraments

The sacraments of the Church portray the Trinitarian character of the life of God and man. Each person is **baptized** by the Holy Spirit into the one humanity of Christ. Being baptized, each person is given the "seal of the gift of the Holy Spirit" of God in **chrismation**

145

to be a "christ", i.e. an anointed son of God to live the life of Christ.

In **marriage** the unity of two into one makes the new unity a reflection of the unity of the Trinity, and the unity of Christ and the Church. For the family of many persons united in one truth and love is indeed the created manifestation of the one family of God's Kingdom, and of God Himself, the Blessed Trinity.

In **penance** once more we renew our new life as sons of the Father through the grace of Christ by the power of the Holy Spirit, forgiven and reunited into the unity of God in His Church.

In **holy unction** the Spirit anoints the sufferer to suffer and die in Christ and so to be healed and made alive with the Father for eternity.

The **priesthood** itself, the ministry of the Church, is nothing other than the concrete manifestation in the Church of the presence of Christ by the same Holy Spirit who makes accessible to all men the action of the Father and the way to everlasting communion in and with Him.

Finally, the "mystery of mysteries," the **Holy Eucharist**, is the actual experience of all Christian people led to communion with God the Father by the power of the Holy Spirit through Christ the Son who is present in the Word of the Gospel and in the Passover Meal of His Body and Blood eaten in remembrance of Him. The very movement of the Divine Liturgy— towards the Father through Christ the Word and the Lamb, in the power of the Holy Spirit—is the living sacramental symbol of our eternal movement in and toward God, the Blessed Trinity.

Even Christian prayer is the revelation of the Trinity, accomplished within the third person of the Godhead. Inspired by the Holy Spirit, men can call God "our Father" only because of the Son who has taught them and enabled them to do so. Thus, the true prayer of Christians is not the calling out of our souls in earthly isolation to a far-away God. It is the prayer in us of the divine Son of God made to His Father, accomplished in us by the Holy Spirit who himself is also divine.

> For we have received the Spirit of adoption, whereby we cry Abba! Father! The Spirit itself bears witness that we are children of God....for we know not what we should pray for as we ought; but the Spirit itself intercedes for us... (Romans 8:15-16, 26)

The Holy Trinity in Christian Life

The new commandment of Christian life is "to be perfect as your heavenly Father is perfect" (Matthew 5:48) It is to love as Christ himself has loved. "This is my commandment, that you love one another as I have loved you." (John 15:12) Men cannot live the Christian life of divine love in imitation of God's perfection without the grace of the Holy Spirit. With the power of God, however, what is impossible to men becomes possible. "For with God all things are possible." (Mark 10:27)

The Christian life is the life of God accomplished in men by the Spirit of Christ. Men can live as Christ has lived, doing the things that he did and becoming sons of God in Him by the power of the Holy Spirit. Thus, once more, the Christian life is a Trinitarian life.

By the Holy Spirit given by God through Christ, men can share the life, the love, the truth, the freedom, the goodness, the holiness, the wisdom, the knowledge of God Himself. It is this conviction and experience which has caused the development in the Orthodox Church of the affirmation of the fact that the essence of Christianity is "the acquisition of the Holy Spirit" and the "deification" of man by the grace of God, the so-called **theosis**.

The saints of the Church are unanimous in their claim that Christian life is the participation in the life of the

Blessed Trinity in the most genuine and realistic way. It is the life of men becoming divine. In the smallest aspects of everyday life Christians are called to live the life of God the Father which is communicated to them by Christ, the Son of God, and made possible for them by the Holy Spirit who lives and acts within them.

The Holy Trinity in Eternal Life

At the end of the ages Christ will come in the glory of God the Father, He will make the Father known throughout all creation. The Holy Spirit will fill all things and enable all to be in union with God through Christ for eternity. Again we have the presence and action of the Holy Trinity.

What we know and experience now in the world as members of the Church will be manifested in power in the life of the kingdom to come. The essence of life everlasting is the life of the Holy Trinity, the same eternal life given to us already in the mystery of faith.

> And I saw no temple in the city, for the Lord God Almighty and the Lamb (Christ) are the temple of it. And the city had no need of the sun...for the glory of God did lighten it, and the Lamb (Christ) is the light thereof...
>
> And the throne of God and the Lamb (Christ) shall be in it, and his servants shall see him..and they shall see his face...
>
> And the Spirit and the Bride (the Church) say Come! (Revelation 21:22; 22:3, 17)

In the eternal life of the Kingdom of God, the Holy Trinity will fill all creation: the Father through the Son in the Holy Spirit. Every man enlightened by Christ in the Spirit will know the invisible Father. "And this is eternal life, that they may know thee the only true God, and Jesus Christ whom thou hast sent." (John 17:3) Such knowledge is possible only by the indwelling of the Spirit of God, "the fullness of Him who fills all in all." (Ephesians 1:23; 2:22)

Come O Ye People! Let us adore the Three-Personal Godhead, the Son in the Father with the Holy Spirit.

For before all time the Father gave birth to the Son, co-eternal and co-enthroned with Himself.

And the Holy Spirit was in the Father, glorified with the Son.

Adoring One Power, One Essence, One Divinity, Let us cry:

O Holy God who made all things by the Son through the cooperation of the Holy Spirit!

O Holy Mighty through whom we know the Father and through whom the Holy Spirit comes into the world!

O Holy Immortal, the Spirit, the Comforter, who proceeds from the Father and rests in the Son!

O Most Holy Trinity! Glory to Thee!

(The Vespers of Pentecost)

SELECTED BIBLIOGRAPHY

Arseniev, Nicholas, *Revelation of LIfe Eternal,* St. Vladimir's Seminary Press, 1962.

Barrois, Georges A., *The Face of Christ in the Old Testament,* St. Vladimir's Seminary Press, 1974.

Bulgakov, Sergius, *The Orthodox Church,* London, Centenary, 1935. Also available in paperback from the American Review of Eastern Orthodoxy, New York, n.d.

Cabasilas, Nicholas, *The Life in Christ,* St. Vladimir's Seminary Press, 1974.

Lossky, Vladimir, *The Mystical Theology of the Eastern Church,* London, James Clarke, 1957.

— *The Vision of God,* London, Faith Press, 1963.

— *In the Image and Likeness of God,* St. Vladimir's Press, 1974.

Meyendorff, John, *The Orthodox Church,* New York, Pantheon Books, 1962.

— *Orthodoxy and Catholicity,* New York, Sheed and Ward, 1966.

— *Christ in Eastern Christian Thought,* St. Vladimir's Seminary Press, 1975.

Pelikan, Jaroslav, *The Spirit of Eastern Christendom (600-1700),* Chicago, The University of Chicago Press, 1974.

Schmemann, Alexander, *For the Life of the World (Sacraments and Orthodoxy),* St. Vladimir's Seminary Press, 1974.

— *Of Water and the Spirit,* St. Vladimir's Seminary Press, 1974.

Ware, Timothy, *The Orthodox Church,* New York, Pelican, 1963.

SELECTED ARTICLES FROM SAINT VLADIMIR'S THEOLOGICAL QUARTERLY

Afanasiev, Nicholas, "The Canons of the Church: Changeable or Unchangeable", *SVQ*, XI,2,1967.

Athenagoras, Metropolitan (Kokkinakis), "Tradition and Traditions", *SVQ*, VII,3,1963.

Basil, Archbishop (Krivosheine), "Is a New Orthodox 'Confession of Faith' Necessary?", *SVQ*, XI,2,1967.

Barrois, George, "The Antinomy of Tradition", *SVQ*, XIII,4,1969.

Bobrinskovy, Boris, "Ascension and Liturgy", *SVQ*, III,4,1959.

Bogolepov, Alexander, "Which Councils are Recognized as Ecumenical?", *SVQ*, VII,2,1963.

Clement, Olivier, "Science and Faith", *SVQ*, X,3,1966.

Florovsky, Georges, "On the Tree of the Cross", *SVQ*, OS1, 1953.

— "And Ascended into Heaven....", *SVQ*, OS2,1954.

Hopko, Thomas, "The Bible in the Orthodox Church", *SVQ*, XIV,1-2,1970.

Kesich, Veselin, "Criticism, the Gospel and the Church", *SVQ*, X,3,1966.

— "Research and Prejudice", *SVQ*, XIV,1-2,1970.

Kniazeff, Alexei, "The Great Sign of the Heavenly Kingdom and Its Advent in Power" (On the Theotokos), *SVQ*, XII,1-2,1969.

Koulomzin, Nicholas, "Images of the Church in Saint Paul's Epistles", *SVQ*, XIV,1-2,1970.

Meyendorff, John, "Historical Relativism and Authority in Christian Dogma", *SVQ*, XI,2,1967.

— "The Orthodox Concept of the Church", *SVQ*, VI, 2,1962.

— "Tradition and Traditions", *SVQ*, VI,3,1962.

— "Doctrine of Grace in St. Gregory Palamas", *SVQ*, S2,1954.

Romanides, John, "Original Sin According to St. Paul", *SVQ*, OS4,1-2,1955-56.

Schmemann, Alexander, "Ecclesiological Notes", *SVQ*, XI,1,1967.

Verhovskoy, Serge, "The Highest Authority in the Church", *SVQ*, IV,2-3,1960.

— "Procession of the Holy Spirit according to the Orthodox Doctrine of the Holy Trinity", *SVQ*, OS2,1953.

— "Some Theological Reflections on Chalcedon", *SVQ*, II,1,1958.